Ministerial Leadership
in a
Managerial World

Ministerial Leadership

IN A

Managerial World

BRUCE W. JONES

Tyndale House
Publishers, Inc.
Wheaton, Illinois

Scripture quotations, unless otherwise noted, are
from the *New American Standard Bible,* copyright
1960, 1962, 1963, 1971, 1973 by The Lockman
Foundation. Scripture quotations marked TLB are
from *The Living Bible,* copyright 1971 held by
assignment to Illinois Regional Bank N.A. (as
trustee). All rights reserved.

First printing, September 1988

Library of Congress Catalog Card Number 88-50702
ISBN 0-8423-3864-0
Copyright 1988 by Bruce W. Jones
All rights reserved
Printed in the United States of America

To my dear wife, Beth,
and our children,
Marilyn, David, and Jonathan

CONTENTS

INTRODUCTION

In 1986 a regional director for the Small Business Administration reported that there were 15 million small businesses in the United States. He described them as "the engine of our economy" because they provide sixteen out of every twenty new jobs. From 1984 to 1986 over 2 million new business ventures were started. Five years after their inception, however, 80 percent of them will fail. The SBA director said that the main reason for their failure would not be insufficient money—it would be inadequate management.

In late 1982 Harper and Row published its number one best-seller in its 157-year history, and it sold 3,400 copies a day. That book, *In Search of Excellence,* described eight basic principles utilized by some of America's biggest and best-run corporations. Even ministers and Christian leaders were encouraged to read it because it contained some biblical principles that should be applied just as much in the church world as in the corporate world. Its 1985 sequel, *A Passion for Excellence,* spoke further of the critical role that the "leadership difference" plays in the pursuit of excellent performance.

Since 1982 some corporate stars within the Fortune 500 constellation have fallen, while others have risen to new heights. People Express Airlines, named an excellent company, took a nosedive while other companies, like Chrysler, rode on to new avenues of success. The primary reason was leadership.

With all of the resources today, why aren't more managers better able to lead their companies on to excellence? Many reasons are offered, but two suggested solutions deserve comment, as they may also be applicable to the ministry. The first of these is the matter of *education prior to experience.* Each year over 60,000 MBAs leave their halls of learning to land jobs paying as much as $60,000 per year. But the authors of *Leaders: The Strategies for Taking Charge* say, "The gap between management education and the reality of leadership in the workplace is disturbing to say the least."[1] In a *Harvard Business Review* article entitled "The Myth of the Well-educated Manager," the author seriously questions the ability of management education programs to develop leadership. Despite the benefit of top teachers, tested textbooks, and tough case studies and tests, the academic achievement models do not provide a valid measurement of real management potential. Management students who have top academic grades have not always passed the test of field experience. Why? Because leadership involves *people* skills, not just *problem-solving* skills. The classroom can't always provide the conditions that test these characteristics, and some experts are advocating that changes be made in the educational systems that prepare people for their leadership roles.

Another reason suggested for the failure of management is the need for *more experience prior to education.* In one of his talks to British managers, Peter Drucker said, "I do not believe in management education for people without substantial business experience. It is a waste and nonsense. I believe in the education of experienced men who have had five years of knowing what work is." No wonder continuing education has become so popular today. Seminars, success motivation tapes, best-seller business books, and corporate consultants are available in abundance to seasoned managers who have not learned all the answers but have learned to ask many of the right questions.

Both of the factors mentioned above are relevant to the world of secular managers. The same can also be said about a host of ministers who are spiritual managers in the church today. How much education and experience do they receive to make them better managers in their ministry?

In their book *The Christian Executive*, Ted Engstrom and Edward Dayton make the observation that "too many Christian organizations are led by men and women who have the gift for ministry and little training (or perhaps even inclination) for management."[2] I once discussed this subject with an executive vice-president of the Sudan Interior Mission. He told me that for a long time mission leaders had reacted to management training, but in 1970 he joined the American Management Association. Since then, he has developed a management course for missionaries and has become convinced he can increase their ministry effectiveness at least 30 percent through basic management training.

When I entered the pastoral ministry over twenty years ago, I was committed to preach the Word, win souls for Christ, serve the Lord, and lead my church. While I am grateful for a good Bible college education and seminary experience, I discovered a decade later what many other ministers have discovered: Ministry involves far more management of people and programs than we have anticipated. Having learned this, I began the next decade in search of expertise in the management of ministry, particularly as it would be more conducive to church growth. When I finished my doctoral studies and a concurrent five-year term as a denominational secretary of evangelism and church growth in 1981, I considered a thesis subject which included some of the topics covered in this book. I did not feel my professional or personal education in management was adequate for the task, so I postponed my writing on the subject. Over a year ago, the Lord encouraged me to author a book on the basis of what I had learned thus far. Beginning with a simple National Association of Evangelicals workshop on the topic "Minister or Manager?" I am now delighted to have completed the book you are about to read.

My general purpose in this book is to provide some church growth guidelines to help pastors be more effective in the management of their ministries. Briefly stated, I also have three specific objectives. First of all, I want to *scripturally synthesize insights from the world of professional management and the work of pastoral ministry.* Some authors rightly argue that the bottom line in the church is people, whereas the bottom line in a corporation is profit. Others also point out that the church is a voluntary organization, whereas companies can hire and fire employees at will. Even so, I hope to show that there are many management concepts that apply to the ministry.

A second objective I have is to *stimulate investigation.* While I have not had the privilege of professional management education, I have tried to read and research the subject and include many references to which the interested reader can refer. I have also sought to utilize relevant church growth literature that might be of particular importance to a minister wanting more information on a particular idea.

A third objective I have in mind is to *provide "seed thought" information.* It is impossible in a book this size to fully discuss different dimensions of management, even though I would like to. It was necessary in some chapters, such as the one on style, to deal with the concept in survey form. In other chapters, like the one on situation, I could only briefly summarize some features of marketing that might be applied to the ministry. I hope readers will not only discover new answers for old questions they have had but will also discover new topics of thought they haven't done much thinking on.

The outline of the book is simple. Because in the minds of many ministers management and ministry do not mix, I have devoted Section One to a Theory of Management that I believe is biblically based, even though it is more broadly built on the principles and philosophy of effective leadership. Section Two is a Typology of Management that includes six critical concepts that are fundamental to the growth of the local church.

Many years ago I heard Bishop Fulton Sheen close a television program with a classic comment. He said, "I would like to thank my writers: Matthew, Mark, Luke, and John!" As I wrote this book, I felt indebted to many who have contributed to my understanding of what I would call ministerial management. Professors who have expounded from their podiums, or in print, the principles of church growth leadership, as well as pastors who have exemplified growth patterns in their local churches, have all enhanced my own understanding and effectivenesss in Christian service. So have writers from the field of management. Many of their ideas and insights are quoted or restated in these pages. I will also be grateful for responses to this book which will test and teach me truth on this theme. I am eager to learn more about leadership in the laboratory of life.

Most of all, I am grateful to my Lord Jesus Christ who has called me to the sacred task of ministry in His church and given me the privilege through the publisher to submit this book to others who desire as I do to be more effective ministers or managers for Him who said, "I will build My church."

NOTES

1. Warren Bennis and Burt Nanus, *Leaders: The Strategies for Taking Charge* (New York: Harper & Row, 1985), 218.
2. Ted W. Engstrom and Edward R. Dayton, *The Christian Executive* (Waco, Tex.: Word, 1979), 16.

SECTION ONE
The Mingling of
Minister and Manager:
A Theory of Management

ONE

CAN THE
CORPORATE BRASS
TEACH THE PASTOR?

THE THEME OF MANAGEMENT

In order to explore management theory and its relationship to the ministry, there are four basic questions we must seek to answer. The first question is, How does the task of ministry relate to the *theme* of management? Some "sub-questions" under this might include the following: Can preaching the gospel to reach the world and planning goals with a PERT chart in the church boardroom both be part of a pastor's ministry? Can soul-winning and a systems analysis of the church organization both be legitimate aims on the church leader's agenda? Is it possible to synthesize our ecclesiology (theology of the church) and current business expertise without violating the Word of God? Can ministry and management ever be united together in holy wedlock, or must they be engaged in an unalterable deadlock?

There are three responses to these questions that Christians and churches might adopt. The first is the view that ministry and management are *mutually exclusive.* There are those who say we should not think of management or business methods when we think of the spiritual ministry of the church. A godly missionary returned some years ago from a life of service on foreign fields and was astonished at the administrative sophistication that had developed in his home church. From his point of view the church was not being spiritual when it used secular management methods. They didn't need organizational renewal, revitalization, or re-development—they needed revival!

The second response is the view that ministry and management can *coexist* in the work of the church. But they are not, and never will be, in a position of equal partnership. The ministry must always be primary while management is secondary. Pastors must always be careful that their management of the church is a complement to their ministry, not a competitor with it. Pastors who are burdened down with running bulletins, buses, or busy errands wonder where these items are in the fine print of their divine contracts or call to the ministry.

The third point of view, which I propose in this book, is that management, properly understood and executed, is a *function* of biblical ministry. However, acknowledgment of management as integral to ministry is not a wholesale endorsement of all the motives and methods of the modern management world. I am not committed to pragmatism without principle. But I am convinced that, all other things being equal, the way a minister manages his church (or the way a church chooses to manage itself) will either help or hinder the growth and success of that church. This is the fundamental assumption of this book. Some of the biblical foundations for my perspective can be seen in the following discussion of all three points of view.

VIEW ONE: MANAGEMENT AND MINISTRY ARE MUTUALLY EXCLUSIVE

Although there may be a few with an Amish point of view, the church at large has accepted and adopted the *technology* of the modern world to help fulfill its mission. We can drive across town or fly around the world to preach the gospel. We can reach out and touch people through the telephone. We can telemarket our ministries, do televisitation, provide dial-a-prayer, or open church hot lines to people in need. One denomination can direct-dial over 70 percent of its foreign missionaries in less than one minute. Christian radio and television can broadcast the Good News through satellite stations.

The Word of God has now been translated on Wycliffe computers and read in hundreds of languages. The "old, old story" has been told on audiocassettes, and there is new technology used in the videocassette industry. It has been estimated that over 30 percent of American homes own a VCR, and customers are buying them at the rate of one million per month. This 5 billion dollar a year business has produced fifteen thousand video titles for public purchase or rental (half of which are pornographic in content). An alert church can use video for training seminars, Bible correspondence courses, evangelistic home shows, or ministries to shut-ins. Via video vignettes, missionaries could visit all their supporting churches four times a year rather than just once every four years. The creative use of technology offers us many tools for our ministry.

But what about the *techniques* of modern management? Are there Christian management techniques as opposed to non-Christian techniques? *Christian Leadership Letter* takes the position that

> although modern western management theory and training is useful in the Christian enterprise, there is (or should be) a qualitative difference in the results of good management within the Christian organization. There may not be Christian management techniques, as such, but manage-

ment techniques used by Christians will produce different results within a Christian organization than those same techniques used in a secular organization.[1]

I tend to agree with that. Various kinds of management techniques can often be effectively used by God in Christian organizations. One example I will examine in detail in a later chapter is the practice of goal-setting. One author who allows for the Christian "baptism" of management techniques is Richard G. Hutchinson, who says, "The Holy Spirit in goal achievement is integral to the church's basic organizational understanding of itself."[2] Hutchinson points out in his book *Wheel within the Wheel* that organizational theory, by definition, assumes that *all* organizations exist for goal-seeking purposes. This, of course, assumes the church is an organization. *Is* the church an organization?

There are some who reject the idea of the church as an organization, so they claim the task of management is not valid for the minister. It is said by some that the church is an organism, not an organization.

Two leading advocates of the idea that the church is an organism and not an organization are Lawrence Richards and Clyde Hoeldtke, authors of *A Theology of Church Leadership*. Hoeldtke, a successful businessman and elder in his church, says, "Our church is Christ's body and not an organization requiring management. . . . As an elder who is gifted in pastoring, I am learning *not* to be a manager."[3] Since for them the church, as His body, is an organism, it is not called to administrate but rather minister to people. Its focus is on people, not programs. Its leadership is the Lord Jesus, no one else. It has no organizational tasks on its agenda, and it must not function as an enterprise. They say, "There is no such thing as a Christian organization."[4] The kind of order in an organization and the kind of order in an organism are intrinsically and essentially different. Norman Shawchuck concurs: "Body leadership and body functions are distinctly different from leadership and functions in an organization. To confuse body and enterprise, organism and organization, is to do violence to the very nature of the church."[5]

A simple analysis clearly shows both the church's organism and organization. The body, as an organism, is orchestrated by a very elaborate and well-defined organization that God the Creator-Designer has placed there. If we also take the analogy of Christ as the Head of His body, the church, according to Ephesians 4:11-16, He is managing the ministry of the church through His Spirit and His saints who are equipped for this purpose. As Ted Engstrom has observed, the church is, in fact, "the most complicated and sophisticated organism in the world."

In his book *Church Growth and the Word of God*, Alan Tibbett pointed out that a healthy church really needs to grow in three dimensions. First of all, it needs to grow *quantitatively*, that is, in numbers. The Book of Acts is very candid in recording the number of converts that were added to the church, and its church growth statistics were often phenomenal. Next, of course, the church and all of its members need to grow *qualitatively*, that is, in the grace and knowledge of our Lord Jesus Christ. We find that the gifts mentioned in Ephesians 4 and elsewhere are given for the perfecting of the saints and for the work of the ministry. In addition, the church must also grow *organically*, that is, as an organization.

As an example, in Acts 6 a problem arose: Some Greek widows needed an equitable distribution of food. For this reason, the apostles appointed and organized deacons in Jerusalem to take care of that responsibility while they themselves continued in prayer and the Word of God. Later, as other churches were established, we find that, according to Acts 20:28, further organiza-

21

tion developed as elders were appointed to be overseers or administrators "to shepherd the church of God which He purchased with His own blood."

There are biblical precedents cited for an organizational understanding of the church. For example, Norman Shawchuck uses John Calvin's biblical model of the three functions of the pastor: prophet, priest, and king. The New Testament counterpart of the Old Testament king is the pastor as organizational leader. In discussing management, Shawchuck says, "When it is exercised by responsible, caring persons, it has an almost exact corollary in the New Testament. That word is stewardship. . . . The pastor is the primary organizational steward of the local church."[6] His task involves "administering wisely and effectively the resources God has given to the church."[7] According to 1 Timothy 3:4-5, an elder or spiritual leader is required to manage his own household well. "But if a man does not know how to manage his own household, how will he take care of the church of God?" Even the family is a basic unit of organization.

In their discussion of *The Management of Ministry,* Ezra Earl Jones and James D. Anderson divide the leadership role of the minister into three distinctive functions. The first is *spiritual* leadership. This involves the tasks most ministers are trained for—preaching, teaching, counseling, etc. The second is *associational* leadership. This involves other ministerial tasks required to care for the church and its people, seen as a voluntary organization. The third is *organizational* leadership. This involves the bureaucratic tasks required for managing an efficient organization.

While disagreeing with some of the specifics of the paradigm, I find their analysis very insightful. They admit that, at the local church level, it is often hard to distinguish where organizational management ends and associational leadership begins. Many times "actual leadership behavior will be accomplishing both functional ends."[8] In their opinion, where any one of these leadership functions is missing or weak, the ministry of the pastor and church will suffer. I agree. *The church is both an organism and an organization.* A careful discernment of both dimensions will be essential for effective ministry. A pastor who views management as antithetical to ministry has both an unbiblical and impractical view of his task. If this task of management is to be part of a pastor's ministry, what kind of partnership should it be?

VIEW TWO: MANAGEMENT AS SECONDARY TO MINISTRY

The suburban pastors that Jones and Anderson studied divided their time in this way: 10 percent to spiritual leadership, 30 percent to organizational leadership, and 60 percent to associational leadership. Various factors can affect the distribution of duties. Whether a church is rural, urban, or suburban is important, as is its size. So is the structure of the congregation, its support staff, and the leadership style and priorities of the pastor. And, of course, as we shall see in Chapter 2, we have to deal with the subject of definition when we describe the responsibilities of organizational leadership. Though a detailed job description for the pastor is subject to many variables, what have ministers and churches generally expected the agenda to include?

Research reveals that many congregations and denominations do not place what is called "administration" high on the pastor's priority list. One sample survey listed seven functions congregations wanted their pastor to perform, and administration was sixth on the list. Other studies also reveal that denominations, by reason of their ecclesiology and traditions, often determine the role model of their pastors in this regard. One such study done by a denominational seminary and published in their denominational magazine revealed two interesting perspectives regarding the expectations of their people. One was that the least valued ministerial functions were administration and leadership. A corollary to this was that they did not want autocratic pastors. And yet church growth pastors are often effective administrators and strong leaders.

In 1956 Samuel W. Blizzard wrote a landmark article entitled "The Minister's Dilemma." He described six practitioner roles to distinguish the work of a minister: preacher, pastor, teacher, priest, administrator, and organizer. As administrator, the pastor was to manage his parish, a role that was considered newer to church practice than the others. In his study of almost seven hundred pastors, he discovered some interesting things.

1. Regarding the *importance* of being an administrator, it was rated last by the pastors.
2. Regarding their sense of *effectiveness* as administrators, it was rated next to last.
3. Regarding their *enjoyment* of the tasks, administration was also last.
4. Regarding their *involvement* in the task, about 40 percent of their time was devoted to administration.
5. Regarding their *preparation* for the task, they felt further training to be administrators was their second highest priority.

Their dilemma was the conflict between their normative-motivational perspectives and their functional orientation. According to Blizzard, the average minister faced "basic ambiguities in performing the practitioner roles."[9]

24

In 1974 Donald P. Smith published *Clergy in the Crossfire*. Pastors, he said, were caught in a role conflict between the persons they understood themselves to be and the roles they felt required to play. Referring to Blizzard and other studies on the subject, he also concluded that "clergymen, on the whole, do not like their organizational and administrative responsibilities."[10] Ministers would rather work with ideas in the study than with organizations in the church. Certainly, ministerial training is more cognitive than relational or organizational. According to another analysis he quotes, "In spite of what he says, the minister is really attracted to administrative tasks because they are more tangible and provide more evidence of concrete achievement."[11] Certainly an experienced minister knows he is rated by people on his leadership and management ability more often than his people admit.

In 1980 another study was done entitled "The Ministers of Minneapolis: A Study in Paradox." Reported in *Leadership* magazine by Paul D. Robbins, it reveals some other interesting indicators. First of all, in an age when *Time* magazine said nine out of ten Americans were unhappy with their jobs, in this study, nine out of ten pastors and priests were *very satisfied* in their work. But again, role conflict is revealed as "a sizable number of Minneapolis pastors are unhappy about the amount of time they must put into adminstrative work they neither prefer, desire, nor feel trained to perform."[12] Quoting a survey conducted by George Gallup, Jr., Robbins stated that only 2 percent of the pastors nationally surveyed rated administration as their most important or most satisfying function.

The most recent study I am aware of in this regard is based on a survey taken by *Leadership* magazine and reported in 1983 as "The Needs of Evangelical Christian Leaders in the United States." In regards to the actual ideal ministry emphasis of evangelical leaders, the researchers found the following:

1. The majority of the 300 respondents indicated that preaching and administrative duties were their major focus.
2. The majority of respondents indicated a desire to shift their emphasis from administrative duties to small group discipling and lay leadership training.
3. The second most frequently suggested educational improvement was more training in administrative management skills.
4. The third most frequently suggested educational improvement was more training in human relations, with an emphasis on leadership relational skills.

Regarding the recurrence of problems and their perceived causes, it appeared to the researchers that "the conceptual thread running through each of the most frequently indicated significant problems has to do with expectations. Of those respondents reporting that a lack of time was their major problem, over 50 percent stated unrealistic expectations of their own were a substantial causal component."[13] Some of that problem may be attributable to the pastor's dilemma regarding what most of these studies call his administrative role.

Various solutions might be offered to resolve this problem. The first is the one most suggested in these studies: *retraining*. In addition to some adjustment in present Bible college and seminary training, there is a growing concern for more continuing education that will include management skills for the ministry. The increase of seminars and books on the subject over the past decade is also indicative of this concern.

Another solution is *reevaluation* of the minister's role on a day to day basis. A more detailed definition of administration in these studies would be helpful, and certainly some duties should be dismissed from the pastor's agenda. Parkinson's law says, "Work increases to fill the time available for doing it." Time management and the establishment of priorities are essential. The apostles said they should not leave the Word of God to serve tables (Acts 6:2-4), and ministers may also get too involved in minutiae that would be best left to others.

A third solution is *renegotiation*. Role expectations need to be reevaluated with the congregation. Job descriptions are often not written, not reviewed, or not realistic. Some churches expect their pastors to do seventy hours of work per week. The minister is expected to be almost "omnicompetent" in his ability, "omnipresent" in his availability, and "omnipotent" in his durability.

Sometimes independent consultants, district and executive denominational personnel are available for the renegotiation process. For example, Growth in Ministry is a Lutheran program designed to match pastoral roles with congregational goals.[14] Thirty pastoral activities have been clustered into six major functions that are rated by a factor analysis. According to their definition, *administration* means the management of church finances and the church office, whereas *organization* means the pastor supplies ideas, promotes lay leadership, works within committees, and plans programs. Whatever resources are utilized, a realistic renegotiation of a minister's role as a manager may make him more effective. It will also make his job more enjoyable.

A fourth solution for some is *rejection*. As Olan Hendrix pointed out in his management seminars years ago, when most pastors are faced with the tasks of ministry and management, they usually like to do ministry more than management. However, he also made the point that the neglect of management work leads to the detriment of the organizations the pastors serve as leaders.

A fifth solution is *redefinition* of what words like *leadership, management,* or, especially, *administration* mean, which I will examine in the next chapter. If the pastor needs to delegate some administrative duties or details, that would be good management. But if he wants to reject his role as the principal leader of the church as an organization, this is not only bad but unbiblical management. There is yet another alternative view.

VIEW THREE: MANAGEMENT AS EXPRESSION OF MINISTRY

Though it may seem radical to suggest, I would propose that, properly understood, the biblical roles of ministry and management are essentially just different dimensions of our calling to be pastors and Christian workers. Certainly the job descriptions and role expectations will vary. But the task of leading the church to fulfill its divine purpose is, in fact, biblical management. Pastors are expected by God to enable the "workers" (see 1 Cor. 12:28) in the church to do "the work of the ministry" (see Eph. 4:11-13). As some have pointed out, the word *administrator* has its root meaning in the word *minister.* Many pastors can identify with one experienced pastor who reflected, "Had I been a better manager, I would also have been a better minister, and I would have undoubtedly come closer to accomplishing the more spiritual goals to which I was dedicated."[15] As I have searched the Scriptures and studied church growth, I have come to the conclusion that godly ministry and good management must go hand in hand. Some of the biblical basis for this third point of view can be seen in answers to the following three questions.

What Is the Biblical Practice of Management? In creation, God gave man "dominion" or "rule" over all the earth (Gen. 1:26-30). This delegated authority and accountability is often called *stewardship*. In Bible times, the closest term we have for manager is the word *steward*, a translation of the Greek word *oikonomos*, often used to mean a household manager. He is given the task of running the household and managing the estate of the master to whom he is responsible (Matt. 25:14-26). The parable in Luke 19:11-27 shows stewards can have different levels of responsibilities, as well as different abilities to perform them. There are also different spheres of responsibility to manage, such as the home (1 Tim. 3:4-5) or the church (1 Tim. 5:17).

In the Old Testament there are many examples of godly men who were also good managers or leaders. Joshua and Jehoshaphat were able military commanders. David and Solomon were wise administrators of the kingdom. Joseph and Daniel earned the respect of heathen kings as proficient and professional managers of state affairs. And certainly Nehemiah has captured the attention of many as a model for ministers. Olan Hendrix says the Book of Nehemiah "contains every major management principle we know about today."[16] And many commentators have extracted some of the explicit or implicit principles in this book to show us how to practice biblical management. Consider just a few examples.

In his book, *Hand Me Another Brick,* pastor Chuck Swindoll says Nehemiah is a classic work on effective leadership. He shows the importance of "the prayer principle" when we practice biblical management. Sometimes it's prayer in response to opportunities (Neh. 1:4; 2:5) or at times it's prayer in response to opposition (Neh. 4:4). Swindoll says, "Prayer was the first major step Nehemiah took in the journey to effective leadership."[17] In any case, he must be leader "from the knees up!"

Former pastor Gordon MacDonald sees in Nehemiah an example of "the Peter Principle" (that is, a man rises in an organization past the level of his competency). Nehemiah was an organizer (entrepreneur) but not a governor (manager). MacDonald says,

> This ought to be a primary mark in the management book of every Christian leader. Know when to start, and then know when to get out. One of the tragedies of our day has been the man who gets a Christian movement off the ground but who couldn't keep it off the ground. Thinking himself successful during the first phase of creation, he sticks with the organization into phase two, never realizing the need for a change in the style of leadership.[18]

What Are Some Biblical Principles of Management? Having seen some Old Testament models of good and godly management, let us turn to the New Testament model of our Lord to illustrate a few more principles. In his book, *The Master Plan of Evangelism*, Robert Coleman sees eight principles Jesus used in the discipling of the apostles. They are (1) selection, (2) association, (3) concentration, (4) impartation, (5) demonstration, (6) delegation, (7) supervision, and (8) reproduction.[19]

Certainly everyone knows the *selection* of the right people for the right job is one of the most important management decisions you can make. That's why there are best-selling books on personnel selection and hiring. The pastor of a famous West Coast church once asked me what I had learned about staff selection. I said you needed to be prayerful, patient, and perceptive. When interviewing prospective students, most college representatives tend to make up their minds in the first four minutes. The right staff person is worth waiting for. The Lord Jesus took time for careful and prayerful selection of His "staff" (Luke 6:13).

The second principle Coleman observes is *associ-*

ation. Jesus calls men to be "with Him" (Mark 3:14). He became their model. As Paul was to later say to his disciple Timothy, "The things which you have heard from me in the presence of many witnesses, these entrust to faithful men, who will be able to teach others also" (2 Tim. 2:2). In the ancient guilds and in the skilled trades of today there is the practice of apprenticeship. In the military and in factories there is the practice of on-the-job training (OJT). In the ancient synagogues as well as twentieth-century graduate schools there is the practice of tutorship. In the corporate world today they're talking about mentorship, and, according to *Psychology Today,* the right age for being mentored is between seventeen and thirty-three, probably the age bracket of the apostles.

In a special 1983 edition of *The Harvard Business Review* there appeared an interesting article entitled "Everyone Who Makes It Has a Mentor." In interviews with three successive chief executives of Jewel Companies, F. J. Lunding, appointed successor to the famous John Hancock, stated that he operated by "the first assistant philosophy." This means executive responsibility involves assisting the people down the line to be successful. The boss in any department is the first assistant to those who report to him. He passed this philosophy on to George Clements, who also believed in the mentor philosophy, and who then handpicked the current president, Donald Perkins. For Perkins, sponsorship is like parenthood. He says, "I don't know that anyone has ever succeeded in any business without having some unselfish sponsorship or mentorship, whatever it might be called."[20]

At first glance, this might appear to be an overstatement. However, in the same publication by *Harvard Business Review, Executive Success—Making It in Managment*, there appeared a supporting article entitled "Clues for Success in the President's Job." In inter-

31

views with over thirty top executives, Joseph Bailey found they all had capacities to have learned firsthand from a mentor. Most of the time the mentors were positive models, though occasionally there were some negative examples. In 90 percent of the interviews, these models were successful executives, maybe thirty years older. The author says they all helped the young associates to form, work out, and practice their own patterns of organizational behavior.[21] Someone enabled them to become good managers. The application of this principle alone has tremendous implications for the work of the church.

Is There a Biblical Philosophy of Management? In the book, *The Art of Management for Christian Leaders,* Ed Dayton takes the position that the question seeks to divide sacred and secular, which cannot be done. He says, "I don't think there is a Christian philosophy of management any more than I think there is a Christian philosophy of bus driving."[22] On the other hand, Peter Rudge, in his book *Ministry and Management,* contends we need to apply Christian doctrine to organization and administration so we can, in fact, develop "managerial theology."[23] For Olan Hendrix "the issue is not the spirituality of management, the issue is the spirituality of the man" who manages.[24] As I understand it, a biblical philosophy of management simply evaluates the purposes, people, principles, and practices of a church organization by scriptural standards. As such, I believe there can be a biblical philosophy of management in the broadest sense of the term, even though Christian leaders and pastors will develop distinctive philosophies of management within these broad guidelines.

Pastors have a dual role: They have been called to minister to people as well as to administer the local church. I have found, in my own experience as well as in the observations of others, that being a minister is not an either/or relationship, but, in the truest sense, it is a both/and responsibility. The pastor is both minister and manager.

Not long ago I was in a meeting with some friends of mine, all of whom are experienced executives in evangelical denominations and organizations. As I raised the question as to whether or not good management is an essential expression of God's ministry in the church, they all agreed that it is. One bishop from a Brethren church said he had never seen a man removed from a pastorate for poor preaching, but he had seen many move on because they had done poorly as managers in the church. Others who had counseled local churches in crisis situations said most often the problem was a "leadership crisis" or a "management crisis." There is no doubt in my mind that the task of ministry critically involves the theme of management in effective and growing churches.

NOTES

1. Edward R. Dayton and Ted W. Engstrom, "Christian Management Techniques?" *Christian Leadership Letter* (World Vision International), September 1980, 2.
2. Richard G. Hutchinson, Jr., *Wheel within the Wheel* (Atlanta: John Knox, 1979), 216.
3. Lawrence O. Richards and Clyde Hoeldtke, *A Theology of Church Leadership* (Grand Rapids: Zondervan, 1980), 80.
4. Ibid., 203.
5. Norman Shawchuck, *What It Means to Be a Church Leader* (Indianapolis: Spiritual Growth Resources, 1984), 26.
6. Norman Shawchuck and Alvin J. Lindgren, *Management for Your Church* (Nashville: Abingdon, 1977), 17-18.
7. Ibid.
8. James D. Anderson and Ezra E. Jones, *The Management of Ministry* (New York: Harper & Row, 1978), 82.
9. Samuel W. Blizzard, "The Minister's Dilemma," *Christian Century,* 25 April 1956, 509.
10. Donald P. Smith, *Clergy in the Crossfire: Coping with Role Conflicts in the Ministry* (Philadelphia: Westminster, 1974), 47.
11. Ibid., 50-51.
12. Paul D. Robbins, "The Ministers of Minneapolis: A Study in Paradox," *Leadership,* Winter 1980, 120.

13. Craig W. Ellison and William S. Mattila, "The Needs of Evangelical Christian Leaders in the United States," *Journal of Psychology and Theology* 2, Spring 1983, 33.
14. *Growth in Ministry* (booklet) (Philadelphia: n.p., 1929).
15. Leroy H. Sandburg, "Ad-ministering in the Eighties," in *How to Survive in the Ministry,* ed. William L. Malcomson (Valley Forge, Penn.: Judson, 1982), 38.
16. Olan Hendrix, *Management for the Christian Worker* (Libertyville, Ill.: Quill Publications, 1976), 8.
17. Charles R. Swindoll, *Hand Me Another Brick* (Nashville: Thomas Nelson, 1978), 42.
18. Gordon MacDonald, "Nehemiah and the Peter Principal," *Eternity,* October 1974, 48.
19. Robert Coleman, *The Master Plan of Evangelism* (Old Tappan, N.J.: Fleming H. Revell, 1968).
20. Eliza G. C. Collins and Patricia Scott, "Everyone Who Makes It Has a Mentor," in *Executive Success: Making It in Management, Harvard Business Review,* ed. Eliza G. C. Collins (New York: John Wiley and Sons, 1983), 83-103.
21. Joseph C. Bailey, "Clues for Success in the President's Job," in *Executive Success: Making It in Management,* ed. Eliza G. C. Collins (New York: John Wiley & Sons, 1983), 24-41.
22. Ted W. Engstrom and Howard R. Dayton, *The Art of Management for Christian Leaders* (Waco, Tex.: Word, 1982), 37.
23. Peter R. Rudge, *Ministry and Management: The Story of Ecclesiastical Administration* (New York: Methuen, Tavistock Publications, 1968).
24. Hendrix, *Management for the Christian Worker,* 37.

TWO

WHAT DO YOU MEAN
BY "MANAGER"?

THE TERMINOLOGY OF
MANAGEMENT

How does the task of ministry relate to the *terminology* of management? Many ministers shy away from the term *manager* when applied to their call to the ministry. For some, the word has only worldly connotations. Knowing this, planners of seminars dealing with management topics for Christian leaders may purposely avoid the word in their overall theme or title. Whereas we can have denominational executive secretaries, Christian education administrators, youth directors, church chairmen, and even Sunday school superintendents, there is a reluctance to say that ministers are managers, too. The preference is for biblical titles like *pastor* (although nonbiblical words like *senior, associate,* and *assistant* are OK) or a more acceptable term like *spiritual leader*. We need to define our terms and examine the terminology of management, leadership, and entrepreneurship as they are being used today.

THE DEFINITIONS OF
MANAGEMENT AND LEADERSHIP

First of all, what is a manager? According to Peter Drucker, the original meaning of the word on the Ameri-

35

can business scene was simple: "A manager is someone who is responsible for the work of other people."[1] However, in the process of time and organizational development, the words *manager* and *management* have become elastic terms in our vocabulary.

For example, consider some of the titles currently used in the American corporate world to describe the functions of management. Positions may be available in the same company for a *leadman, foreman, shop boss, supervisor, director, manager, administrator, senior vice-president, president,* or even *chairman of the board.* Other executive positions on the management team might include professionals such as a *treasurer* or *company comptroller.* On the other hand, a one-man corner newsstand may be operated by "Bill Johnson—Manager." But he may not own the business or be responsible for the work of others. People at the bank who handle our money may be called *account managers.* People Express made airline headlines with a competitive no-frills pricing system and a strong participatory process of management. Even the stewards and stewardesses who served my wife and me on a flight were all called *service-managers.*

Consider how some of these terms have been defined. According to one glossary, a *manager* is someone who (a) manages the talents of others and (b) normally allows them to determine how they will perform. On the other hand, a *director* is someone who (a) directs others to do his will and (b) gets involved at the level of detail. While this may be a useful guide in principle, in practice we know that there are directors who manage others and there are managers who get involved in the detail work of those they direct. While titles and terms are useful in our understanding of management, they are not always uniform in their application by those they manage.

Second, then, what is a leader? In his classic book,

Leadership, James MacGregor Burns makes two important observations. The first is that "leadership is the most observed and least understood phenomenon on earth."[2] Extensive empirical research has been conducted and multiple management models have been constructed. But with all the accumulated insights and expertise on the subject, behavioral psychologists and organizational analysts have not come to complete agreement on the nature of leadership. Burns also observed that "leadership as a concept has dissolved into small and discrete meanings."[3] More recently, the authors of *Leaders: The Strategies for Taking Charge* said, "Decades of academic analysis have given us more than 350 definitions of leadership."[4] A brief review of a few definitions will not only illustrate the point but point out a critical issue in the concept of leadership.

According to the *Encyclopedia Britannica,* leadership is the exercising of influence over others on behalf of the leader's purposes, aims, or goals. In this definition, the leader says, "Follow me. I know where I'm going!" The president of a democracy or the current dictator of a third world country can operate by this definition. What may distinguish them are their motives and means. The dictator may only want personal power. His means of influence may be fiat command or forceful coercion. The president may want something for the good of his country. His means of influence may be personal popularity, political diplomacy, or persuasive speeches. The Lord Jesus said, "Follow Me," and neither His mission, motives, nor means are in question. In the church world, it may mean the pastor will set the agenda. The pastor of a large, successful church in the South once announced from the pulpit that they were going to initiate an evangelistic calling program. When challenged by some of his board members, he simply replied, "We don't vote on this. It's in the Bible."

Another definition states, "A leader is someone who

succeeds in getting others to follow." In this pragmatic definition, the focus is really on followership, on the individuals being led. Nations, employees, and even church members will follow a leader they consider legitimate. Each group or individual within a group has definite expectations, though, about the qualifications that they consider necessary. Both professional and personal qualifications will be considered in the criteria. If the leader is not legitimate in their eyes, they will express resistance, either actively or passively. During the Vietnam War it was known that some combat units contemplated or carried out the murder of officers they could not trust to lead them in battle. Employees have many passive procedures to minimize their performance when management loses credibility or doesn't care. Within the church, members who oppose pastors or church programs may stop giving or coming to church.

In the church, both theological and sociological perspectives help set the standards by which a minister may "pay his dues" to get accepted. In one middle-class suburban church, a very gifted evangelist resigned. His personal charisma and evangelistic messages each Sunday were a powerful attraction for many to come to the church and to Christ. He was followed by a pastor who loved evangelism but focused his pulpit ministry on expository preaching. His invitations were not always evangelistic sermonettes. Shortly after he arrived, one of his leaders resigned because the pastor "did not preach the gospel." The real issue was style, not substance.

In a lumbering community a missionary who came to open closed churches found it difficult to establish credibility with the men who grew up there. As an apostolic "tentmaker," he lived with his family for three years in a two-room trailer. Day by day he worked alongside the men, peeling bark off the trees to soften the men's resistance to him as an "outsider." Unfortunately, he was not too successful. The issue, though, was not just spiritual; it was also sociological. A pastor friend in Maine told me that at a funeral of an older man who came to the community as a teenager he heard one lady remark to another, "Well, he really wasn't from this area, was he?" In both cases, success in getting others to follow was contingent on their agenda.

In his book, *Competent to Lead,* Kenneth O. Gangel says, "The history of management science might well be told as a history of the story of role conflict between the individual and the institution, the man and the organization."[5] In technical terms, the leader-manager is challenged to maintain a balance between being institution-oriented (nomothetic) and individual-oriented (ideographic). President Eisenhower defined leadership as the ability to get a person to do what you want him to do, when you want it done, in the way you want it done, because he wants to do it. On the other hand, President Truman said that a leader is a man who has the ability to get other people to do what they don't want to do and like it. How this basic organizational issue may be resolved in the church is discussed in later chapters. Meanwhile, it's clear from these two definitions that leadership is at least a dynamic relationship between the goals of leaders and followers.

THE DISTINCTIONS BETWEEN LEADERSHIP AND MANAGEMENT

In July 1977 *Christianity Today* featured an article entitled "Lifting Ministers Out of the Mud" by Ed Dayton. In drawing attention to the fact that there has been an increased interest in management among ministers, he pointed out that there is a difference between running a church like a business and running it like an organization. In a letter to the editor that followed, he was criticized for what the letter's writer considered the error of treating leadership and management as synonymous. The layman said leadership has to do with people and management has to do with things. There are, indeed, distinctions, and one management consultant on the American Management Association seminar circuit advertises that if you want to climb to an annual income exceeding $100,000, the first necessary step is to make the critical distinction between leadership and management.

In his book *The Making of the Christian Leader*, Ted Engstrom says,

> When I use the term *leader*, I see him as one who guides and develops the activities of others. This includes the president, administrator, executive, pastor, director, superintendent, supervisor, department head, and so on. It is a broader term than the popular term *manager*, which traditionally is associated more with industry or commerce.[6]

There is a real sense in which leadership can be exercised in areas where management per se is not really the focus. Someone can be the leader of a street gang, a high school class clique, a moral crusade, a political revolution, a spiritual reformation, or even a sports team. In a local church there are opinion-makers who may not hold specific positions of influence to manage the affairs of the church, but they manage to influence the church as leaders.

Sometimes in the corporate world leadership is viewed as a function of management. In "The Management Process in 3-D," R. Alec MacKenzie says there are three types of managers in an organization: the planner, the administrator, and the leader. The terms *leader* and *manager* should not be used interchangeably because while good managers may often be good leaders and vice versa, it is not always the case. Turning to the military sector, he shares an example.

> In World War II, General George Patton was known for his ability to lead and inspire men on the battlefield but not for his conceptual abilities. In contrast, General Omar Bradley was known for his conceptual abilities, especially planning and managing a campaign, rather than for his leadership.[7]

This point of view says managers are required to plan and organize, while the primary role of a leader is to influence people. Strong leaders may be weak managers. A weak leader can still be a relatively effective manager if he manages people who are capable and committed to the task. Excellent managers must have reasonably high leadership ability.

When President Kennedy challenged America with the statement, "Ask not what your country can do for you, ask what you can do for your country," he functioned as a leader, not a manager. So did Patrick Henry when he said, "Give me liberty, or give me death!" General Douglas MacArthur did when he told the people of the Philippines, "I shall return." And Martin Luther did when he said, "Here I stand, I can do no other." John Wesley and George Whitefield were both outstanding leaders in the eighteenth-century revival that swept England. The difference between these two men was not just theological (Calvinism versus Arminianism), it was organizational. Wesley was a leader who managed to leave behind a horse, a Bible, and a whole Methodist church. Unlike Whitefield, he was both leader and manager. D. L. Moody, the great evangelist, is often credited as also being a great organizer because of his work with the YMCA and other Christian organizations.

The classic management model called PLOC says

that, in addition to staffing, there are four basic components in competent management: planning, leading, organizing, and controlling. Some ministers and managers are good planners but poor executors. That is why some senior pastors who are good leaders but poor managers will function better with the support of a good church secretary, administrative assistant, church chairman, or associate pastor.

When Peter Drucker first wrote his book, *The Effective Executive* in 1966, he made a distinction between effectiveness and efficiency in organizations. Effectiveness is the ability to get the right things done. Efficiency is the ability to do things right.[8] More recently, the authors of *Leaders* stated, "Leaders do the right things, and managers do things right." They studied ninety top leaders to find out how someone can be an effective leader and not just a manager. In their opinion, most organizations are managed, not led. The distinctive role of leadership is the quest for "know-why" ahead of "know-how." This emphasis seems to be on a perceptive ability more than ability to lead people. But a quick analysis of the authors' four strategies for taking charge shows the need to influence people through (1) vision, (2) persuasive communication of that vision, (3) an atmosphere of trust, and (4) a positive self-regard that empowers others to act. They discovered that this positive leadership of others "turns out to be a pivotal factor in their capacity to lead."[9]

In his book *Leading Your Church to Growth,* Peter Wagner says that every manager needs to be a leader, but not every leader needs to be a manager. Leadership involves concepts, vision, and overall direction. Once these are established, management gets the job done. Regarding pastors and church growth, he says,

> Few pastors are pure leaders or pure administrators. Most are a mix of the two. But I have observed

that pastors who tend toward being leaders, whether or not they are also administrators, will most likely be church growth pastors. Pastors who see themselves to be administrators and use that kind of management style tend to be maintenance-oriented. Making sure that the church functions smoothly and harmoniously is usually where a manager is. A leader, on the other hand, is willing to take risks and upset the status quo in order to move out toward new horizons.[10]

Based on some material originally produced by Olan Hendrix, Ted Engstrom lists other distinctives made between leaders and managers.

LEADERSHIP	MANAGEMENT
• is a quality	• is a science and an art
• provides vision	• supplies realistic perspectives
• deals with concepts	• relates to functions
• exercises faith	• has to do with facts
• seeks effectiveness	• seeks efficiency
• is an influence for good among potential resources	• coordinates resources for maximum accomplishment
• provides direction	• is concerned about control
• thrives on opportunity	• succeeds on accomplishment

From Ted W. Engstrom, *The Making of a Christian Leader* (Grand Rapids: Zondervan, 1976), p. 23. Used with permission.

In 1977 Abraham Zaleznik wrote an article in *Harvard Business Review* entitled "Managers and Leaders: Are They Different?" According to his definition, "leaders create new approaches and imagine new areas to explore."[11] They are on the creative cutting edge. This is what the book *A Passion for Excellence* is all about. In it the authors focus on the leadership difference in successful organizations. Their concept of leadership is so crucial that the authors want to discard the words *managing* and *management* altogether. For them, manage-

	LEADERS	MANAGERS
HOW THEY VIEW THEMSELVES	Leaders see themselves as separate from their organizations and the people of their organizations. Leaders have strong personal mastery which impels them to struggle for change in existing order.	Managers have a strong sense of belonging to their organizations. Managers see themselves as protectors of existing order with which they identify.
HOW THEY VIEW THEIR FUNCTION	Leaders question established procedure and create new concepts. They inspire people to look at options. They are concerned with results.	Managers work through other people within established organizational policies and practice to reach an organizational goal. They limit their choices to pre-established organizational goals, policies, and practices. Managers are concerned with process.
PERSONALITY	Leaders seek out risks, especially where rewards seem high. Leaders dislike mundane tasks.	Managers have a strong instinct for survival. Managers can tolerate mundane, practical work.
RELATIONSHIPS	Leaders relate to people in an intuitive and empathetic way.	Managers relate to people according to their role, that is, boss,

ment has images of restriction, tradition, dispassionate analysis, decision-making, and insensitivity to people. For them, leadership is unleashing energy, building, growing. The leader is a "cheerleader, enthusiast, nurturer of champions . . . coach, facilitator, builder.[12]

Zaleznik says managers are different from leaders in that they want to maintain the balance of operations. They tend to adopt impersonal, if not passive, attitudes

	LEADERS	MANAGERS
RELATIONSHIPS *(continued)*		employee, peer, and so forth.
PRIMARY CONCERN	Leaders are concerned with achievement of personal goals.	Managers are concerned with achievement of organizational goals.
PLACE IN ORGANIZATION	Leaders may be found at any level of the plan of organization from technician to highest echelon.	Managers are supervisors, department heads, administrators. They are usually considered the higher echelon.
POWER	Leaders derive power through personal relationships.	Managers derive power from their positions.
GOALS	Leaders are concerned with personal goals. They are not comfortable with the status quo of established organizational goals and policies. They enjoy innovating.	Managers are concerned with pre-established, organizational goals. Their personal and sub-goals arise out of necessity to conform to organizational structure rather than a desire to change.

From Mary E. Tramel and Helen Reynolds, *Executive Leadership* (Englewood Cliffs, N.J.: Prentice-Hall, 1981), 59-60. Used with permission.

toward goals. Their work is an enabling process for some predetermined plan. They see themsleves as coordinators and regulators of an existing order of affairs. While leaders work from high-risk positions, managers have an instinctive need for survival. He says, "Why one individual seeks risks while another approaches problems conservatively depends more on his or her personality and less on conscious choice."[13]

In fact, he says, "Leaders are of a psychologically different type than managers."[14] But, he is not ready to conclude that it's impossible for one person to be both a leader and a manager at the same time. Certainly these differences can be observed among ministers, too. If ministers reading this book wonder if they are leaders or managers, or both, the authors of *Executive Leadership* have provided an excellent checklist which can guide the reader in making a self-evaluation or having someone else evaluate you.

THE DIFFERENCES BETWEEN MANAGEMENT AND ENTREPRENEURSHIP

According to some experts, we are now living in the age of entrepreneurism, although Peter Drucker says, "The wave of entrepreneurial activity is primarily an American phenomenon."[15] In 1970 there were 90,000 new businesses registered in America. Even though a number of enterprises have failed or filed for bankruptcy since then, in 1985, the search for the American dream continued as 600,000 new business organizations were started. Many of them began as "one-man" operations, and some of them are run out of the homes of enterprising housewives. Magazines such as *Entrepreneur* and *Venture—The Magazine for Entrepreneurs*, are now available for the rising number of new entrepreneurs in America.

However, entrepreneurism today is not just founding and operating one's own business. It's a state of mind and a desirable function within growing corporate structures as well. The new "passion for excellence" advocates consistent innovation and the freedom to take risks. Leadership involves trust and respect for the creative potential of each person in the organization. The American Management Association now says the need for innovative management is greater than ever before. Its goal is to train managers who will enable people to find new and even unusual approaches. Its new monthly newsletter, *Intrepreneural Excellence,* gives practical tips on creativity. "In" words for business book titles now include *create, innovate, entrepreneurship* and *intrepreneurship.*[16]

In the church world there is also evidence of entrepreneurism. There are those who predict that

> the proliferation of para-church ministries and organizations will be one of the distinguishing hallmarks of the last half of the twentieth century. Para-local church groups now number between five and and ten thousand and that number is increasing daily. Some estimates run as high as twenty thousand.[17]

The American Association of Christian Schools in California has now registered almost twenty-five hundred schools, an increase of over a thousand since 1980. In 1985, 195 schools were registered, approximately one school every other day. Peter Drucker says there are two new Christian schools started every day across the nation, but more recently, Dr. Keinel, Executive Director of the American Association of Christian Schools says *three* new schools start every day.

Traditionally, the entrepreneur's unique role is innovation at the outset: the founding of an organization. According to one definition, "Everyone is an entrepreneur only when he actually carries out new combinations and loses that character as soon as he builds up his business."[18] Faced with limited resources and high risks, the pioneer takes up the challenge of a new venture. In a land of almost 340,000 churches, new churches are being started every day. One denomination alone indicates that they start 365 new churches each year, one third of which are ethnic. Another denomination has church planting as its major growth strategy (By Elmer Towns's definition, the church plant-er is someone who can "start a church in the face of insurmountable odds, with limited resources, in unlike-ly circumstances."[19]) Jerry Falwell wants to see the students from Liberty Schools start five thousand new churches by the year 2000. (No wonder graduates like these start a church in a small Massachusetts town and call it the New England Baptist Temple.)

What is the entrepreneur like? According to the book *CEO*, "Entrepreneurs have their own unique psychology."[20] But after years of management consultation experience, Peter Drucker discounts the idea of an "entrepreneurial personality." The common characteristic of entrepreneurs for Drucker is "a commitment to the systematic practice of innovation."[21]

In my opinion, there are several characteristics that describe people who are entrepreneurs at heart. For one, they are challenged by opportunities. In fact, they focus more attention on opportunities than obstacles. They turn their lemons into lemonade. They are "possibility thinkers," not "liability thinkers." When other people ask why, they say, Why not? and When? When they work within organizations, entrepreneurs—who then become *intrepreneurs*—"search the organization and environment for opportunities to initiate improvement projects to bring about change."[22] As managers, they supervise the design and development of new projects as well. The two most important questions they ask are, Is this change *desirable*? and, Is this change *achievable*? In other words, Is the power and ability to meet the goal available?

Another common characteristic is that they desire control. This partially explains their willingness to endure personal sacrifice (e.g., family time) or professional stress. In their study of 450 small business owners, the authors of the article "Coping with Entrepreneurial Stress" found that "independence and freedom of decision making were among the benefits . . . mentioned most frequently."[23] Entrepreneurs are very achievement-oriented, but their passionate pursuit of control may cause problems at two levels of an organization. In regard to *superiors,* one psychoanalyst of management says,

> While managers seem able to identify in a positive and constructive way with authority figures . . . many of the (38) entrepreneurs I have observed lack the manager's fluidity in changing from a superior to a subordinate role. Instead, they often experience structure as stifling. They find it difficult to work with others in structured situations unless, of course, they created the structure and the work is done on their terms.[24]

In regard to *subordinates,* the entrepreneurs' classic problem is often delegation. They may, at times, complain about detail work, but they often delight in it. At times some of them fear or distrust others taking charge of things they control or get the credit for. Entrepreneurial organizations often flounder because the founder can't change his working style. I once observed the founding pastor of a five-hundred-member church involved in the details of setting up the table arrangements for a Sunday school staff dinner. Entrepreneurial pastors who can't delegate administrative responsibility may unwittingly hinder the development of other leaders. Others who are frustrated with the status quo of maintenance-oriented churches might best devote their energies to starting new churches. The third characteristic common to these people is their *creativity and innovation,* which we will consider below in more detail.

How do managers compare to entrepreneurs? In examining "The Heart of Entrepreneurship," a *Harvard*

Business Review article, the authors conclude they have different characteristics than administrators. Within a range of behavior, at one extreme is the promotor-type, the entrepreneur who feels confident of his ability to seize opportunities with limited resources. At the other extreme is the trustee-type who tends to rely on the status quo. The former is pro-active, the latter is re-active. The former wants to create, the latter wants to conserve. The entrepreneur is willing to take risks. The trustee-administrator wants to reduce them.[25] Not all pastors will excel at entrepreneurship. Some studies show that only 5 percent of American pastors invent or design their own programs. As such, many tend to look for prepackaged programs or prefabricated models of church growth. They may attend pastors' schools and seminars to be told how to do it according to the ministerial model presented. They are faithful plodders along well-defined paths rather than pioneers who lead the way.

Sometimes this can produce positive results. One pastor went to a popular evangelism training program with a proven track record, but he returned home to make up his own creative version of the program for his church. After six months, he called the founder of the program to ask why it wasn't working. The founder asked a series of questions about the conformity of the program to the original pattern and concluded by saying, "The reason my program is not working in your church is because you are not working my program, but yours." The pastor returned to the seminar a second time, established the program intact, and saw positive results thereafter.

On the other hand, I know of another pastor who left Bible school with a well-defined methodology for church planting and evangelism. After a short pastorate in a rural community, he left and shook the dust off his feet, convinced the town was incurably hardened to the gospel message he presented. In my judgment, he was partially ineffective because he came as a stranger to a highly relational community and tried to use a very strong confrontational approach in evangelism. Blessed is the minister who knows when to adopt and adapt prepackaged programs for his particular situation.

In conclusion, we should note that another word that sometimes appears in the terminology of management is *administration.* In 1951, Ordway Tead wrote *The Art of Administration,* and defined it as

> the process and agency which is responsible for the determination of the aims for which an organization and its management are to strive, which establishes broad policies under which they are to operate, and which gives general oversight to the continuing effectiveness of the operation.[26]

Today, the executive level of the United States government is still called The Administration by the media. Various books have also been written for the church which continue to use this broad term.[27] However, many of the functions described as administration are more currently described as management, and the term *administration* is not used so widely today. In addition, it would appear from the studies conducted with pastors (discussed in Chapter 1) that administration often focuses on routine, if not mundane, duties or details in office operations. If permitted to use the term as defining more routine procedure, then a summary statement can be attempted.

Given the diversity of definitions available and the broad range of responsibilities possible, it is difficult to conclude with a simple synopsis. The terminology of management can involve a significant spectrum of understanding when applied to the task of ministry. At the risk of oversimplification, the following diagram gives a broad framework of reference for understanding some of the terms reviewed. Good entrepreneurs have some ability in each area.

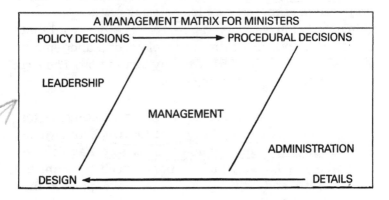

A MANAGEMENT MATRIX FOR MINISTERS

POLICY DECISIONS ──────────▶ PROCEDURAL DECISIONS

LEADERSHIP

MANAGEMENT

ADMINISTRATION

DESIGN ◀────────── DETAILS

How Do You See Yourself?

In the use of this matrix diagram, three assumptions should be made. First, the *size* of an organization or church and the corresponding position held will be variables in how to describe the function. Second, the *style* of individuals will be a variable in describing how they function. And third, the *situation* at the time will be a variable on what function is needed. While any minister may best be described in one of these three dimensions of the management matrix, the same minister may function in all three dimensions at different times in his ministry. The pastoral prism of God's gifts and callings are reflected through a wide spectrum of management functions in the ministry. The church at large needs ministers who may be leaders, managers, or administrators, and also entrepreneurs.

NOTES

1. Peter F. Drucker, *Management: Tasks, Responsibilities, Practices* (New York: Harper & Row, Harper Colophon Books, 1973), 390.
2. James MacGregor Burns, *Leadership* (New York: Harper & Row, Harper Torchbooks, 1978), 2.
3. Ibid.
4. Warren Bennis and Burt Nanus, *Leaders: The Strategies for Taking Charge* (New York: Harper & Row, 1985), 4.
5. Kenneth O. Gangel, *Competent to Lead: A Guide to Management in Christian Organizations* (Chicago: Moody, 1974), 128.
6. Ted W. Engstrom, *The Making of a Christian Leader* (Grand Rapids: Zondervan, 1976), 15.
7. R. Alec MacKenzie, "The Management Process in 3-D," *Harvard Business Review* 47, November 1969, 80.
8. Peter R. Drucker, *The Effective Executive* (New York: Harper & Row, 1967), 4.
9. Ibid., 60.
10. C. Peter Wagner, *Leading Your Church to Growth* (Ventura, Calif.: Regal, 1984), 89.
11. Abraham Zaleznik, "Managers and Leaders: Are They Different?" *Harvard Business Review* 55, May-June 1977, 67-78.
12. Tom Peters and Nancy Austin, *A Passion for Excellence: The Leadership Difference* (New York: Random House, 1985), 266.
13. Zaleznik, "Managers and Leaders," 72.
14. Ibid., 68.
15. Peter R. Drucker, "Our Entrepreneurial Economy," *Harvard Business Review* 62, January-February 1984, 60.
16. Some books that might be of interest to the reader are *Intrapreneurship,* by Clifford Pinchott III (New York: Harper and Row, 1985), *The Changemasters,* by Rosabeth Moss Kantor (New York: Simon and Schuster, 1983), and *Innovation and Entrepreneurship Principles and Practices,* by Peter F. Drucker (New York: Harper and Row, 1985).
17. Jerry White, *The Church and the Parachurch: An Uneasy Marriage* (Portland, Ore.: Multnomah, 1983), 35.
18. Henry Mintzberg, *The Nature of the Managerial Work* (New York: Harper & Row, 1973), 13.
19. Elmer Towns, *Getting a Church Started in the Face of Insurmountable Odds, with Limited Resources, in Unlikely Circumstances* (Nashville: Impact, 1975).
20. Henry Levinson and Stuart Rosenthal, *CEO: Corporate Leadership in Action* (New York: Basic Books, 1984).
21. Peter F. Drucker, "The Discipline of Innovation," *Harvard Business Review* 63, May-June 1985, 67.
22. Mintzberg, *Nature of Managerial Work,* 93.
23. David P. Boyd and David E.Gumpert, "Coping with Entrepreneurial Stress," *Harvard Business Review* 61 (March-April 1983), 46.
24. Manfred F. R. Kets deVries, "The Dark Side of Entrepreneurship," *Harvard Business Review* 63 (November-December 1985), 161.

25. Howard H. Stevenson and David E. Comport, "The Heart of Entrepreneurship," *Harvard Business Review* 63 (March-April 1985), 39.
26. Ordway Tread, *The Art of Administration* (New York: McGraw-Hill, 1951), 101.
27. Some sample titles include *Foundations for Purposeful Church Administration,* by Alvin J. Lindgren (Nashville: Abingdon, 1965), *Creative Church Administration,* by Lyle E. Schaller and Charles E. Tidwell (Nashville: Abindgon, 1975), and *Church Staff Administration,* by Leonard E. Wedel (Nashville: Abingdon, 1978).

Three

HOW DO WE USE
THE GIFTS?

THE THEOLOGY OF MANAGEMENT

How does the ministry relate to the *theology* of management? Is there a biblical theology to support the
thesis that ministers are managers, too? Some would
say no. In *A Theology of Church Leadership* the authors
say, "The emerging picture of the local church leader. . .
is not that of the manager of an enterprise or a decision-
maker."[1] But I believe a New Testament study of the
responsibilities of the management roles in the church
and the resources of the management gifts given the
church provide a positive answer to that question. A
prerequisite to that study is the establishment of some
perspectives that pertain to spiritual gifts.

Spiritual gifts and natural talents are both a part of a
biblical theology of management. In chapter 2 I tried to
identify some of the distinguishing characteristics of
leaders, managers, and entrepreneurs, characteristics
that might be true of a secular man or a spiritual man.
From a biblical view, all natural talents are given man
by God the Creator. Prior to birth, Jeremiah was set
apart by God to be a "tender" prophet (Jer. 1:5), and

John the Baptist was filled with the Spirit in his mother's womb (Luke 1:15) to be a "thundering" prophet.

All men should say of God with the psalmist, "Thou didst form my inward parts; Thou didst weave me in my mother's womb" (Ps. 139:13). Warren Wiersbe once said it was in his "genetic code" to be some things in life, but not a mechanic or an athlete. Each man inherits some potential that needs to be developed. According to *Christian Leadership Letter,* "There is growing evidence that each of us has a set of characteristics that are more or less fixed early in life."[2] They peak between the ages of seventeen and twenty-two. The definition of a natural talent is an inherited or learned ability which enables a person to perform certain tasks. When Paul says to the Christians in Corinth, "What do you have that you did not receive?" (1 Cor. 4:7), he includes those inborn qualities.

Natural talents may be dedicated to God (Rom. 12:1) but not necessarily used significantly in ministry. John Wimber, who used to head up the Fuller Department of Church Growth, was a professional musician prior to his conversion. He was not at that time called into a music ministry, although he uses his musical talent in ministry today. Peter Wagner said of him, however, that "God took his natural talent as a salesman and transformed that into the gift of evangelism."[3]

The Bible teaches that only those who are "born again" (John 3:1-16) receive spiritual gifts (1 Cor. 12:1-7) for the "common good" and "edification" of the church (1 Cor. 12:12, 26; Eph. 4:12). But opinions are divided over the relationship of talents given to us naturally and gifts given to us supernaturally.

Some take the view that spiritual gifts should *not* be regarded as just an enlargement of natural powers. In their book on the gift of faith, Jerry Falwell and Elmer Towns state, "A spiritual gift is *not* the augmented natural ability of a Christian."[4] On the other hand, Wagner takes the view that while spiritual gifts are not to be regarded as natural, there may be a discernible relationship between the two. "In some cases God takes a natural talent in an unbeliever and transforms it into a spiritual gift when that person enters the body of Christ."[5] W. A. Criswell also believes that natural gifts originally found in human nature can be elevated and enlarged by the addition of gifts of the Spirit. Many of the older commentators on spiritual gifts used to say they were distributed according to "the confirmation which each one received by nature." This may be sometimes true, but not always. Billy Graham says, "It appears that God can take a talent and transform it by the power of the Holy Spirit and use it as a spiritual gift . . . the difference is frequently a cause of speculation by many people. I am not sure we can always draw a sharp line between spiritual gifts and natural talents—both of which come ultimately from God."[6]

Christians can be "multi-gifted." A few writers, like Gene Getz, believe in a multigifted church rather than a multigifted man. But most writers are multiple-gifted rather than mono-gifted in their view. (See 1 Cor. 12:1-4; Matt. 25:15.) Wagner calls this a person's "gift-mix" and makes the observation that "given the varieties of gifts, the degree of giftedness in each one, the multiple ministries through which each gift can be exercised, the combination of these qualities . . . may be the most important factor in determining our spiritual personalities."[7]

Spiritual gifts, like natural talents, can be developed to varying degrees of effectiveness. And finally, effectiveness for a Christian requires that our motive be for the glory of God and that our ministry be performed in the power of the Spirit. A graphic summary of these perspectives can be seen in the following chart.

	NATURAL MAN	SPIRITUAL MAN	CARNAL MAN
1. PROVIDER	God	Holy Spirit	Either
2. PLACEMENT	Talents	Spiritual Gifts	Either
3. POINT IN TIME	Natural Birth	New Birth	Either
4. PURPOSE	Self	Service	Either
5. POWER	Natural	Supernatural	Natural

THE RESPONSIBILITIES OF THE MANAGEMENT ROLE

It is clear from the New Testament that some men are called by God to give leadership in the local church. Hebrews 13 refers three times (vv. 7, 17, 24) to "those who rule." This is a translation of the Greek word *hegeomai* which means "to take the lead." Another word found in 1 Thessalonians 5:12 and 1 Timothy 5:17 is *proistemi* which literally means "to stand before" and is also translated "rule" or "have charge over you." Apart from these general references, there are three terms used to describe the office of minister. They are *elder* (used sixteen times), *overseer* or *bishop* (used six times), and *pastor* (used three times). Sometimes the terms are used interchangeably. In Acts 20:17, Paul sends for the elders of the Ephesian church and charges them, "Be on guard for yourselves and for all the flock among which the Holy Spirit has made you overseers to shepherd the church of God which He purchased with His own blood" (Acts 20:28). "I exhort the

58

elders among you . . . shepherd the flock of God among you, taking the oversight thereof" (1 Pet. 5:1-2). It is generally admitted by scholars that in the early church these three titles refer to the ministry of one and the same person. The meaning of these terms in the New Testament sheds light on the ministry of management for today.

The Office of Elder. Based on the Jewish tradition, the leaders of the local church are often called *elders* and appear early in the development of Christianity (Acts 11:30; 14:23). Every Jewish synagogue had elders, whose origin is traced back to Moses' appointment of seventy men in Numbers 11:16. They presided over the worship services, administered discipline, and even settled disputes as law courts for their people. The Greek word is *presbuteros*, which means simply "older man" or "elder." In 1 Timothy, Paul sets the scriptural standards for this office, and later says, "Let the elders who rule well be considered worthy of double honor, especially those who work hard at preaching and teaching" (1 Tim. 5:17).

In some church traditions, *elders* means the lay leadership of the congregation. Many free church denominations (many Baptists, for example) use the word *deacon* for the same function, although some retain the word *elder* as well. In the Reformed tradition, the pastor is the "teaching elder" and the laymen who administer or manage the church are called the "ruling elders." In April 1976 *Eternity* magazine reported that many Reformed and Presbyterian leaders were coming to feel that there is only one order of elders, and every elder was directed by Scripture to both rule and teach. Many scholars will support the view that all elders are responsible "to rule," even though some of them have special gifts as pastors to work hard at preaching and teaching.

An unbiblical dichotomy between those elders who minister the Word and those elders who manage the work can cause management problems in the ministry of the church. In one church with a large multiple staff, the elders decided they wanted to discontinue their monthly meeting with the staff and meet only with the senior pastor. I see at least three problems with this. First of all, from an organizational point of view, this would have placed an undue and unnecessary burden on the senior pastor as the single communication link between the elders, the associate pastor who served as an executive pastor on the staff, and the rest of the pastoral staff. Second, from a psychological point of view, it seemed to discount or demean the collective education and experience of a pastoral staff who had spent many man-hours in the ministry. Third, from a scriptural point of view, it placed the elders above the pastoral staff, many of whom were just as much called and qualified to be elders as they. When the decision was reversed, they avoided what I believe to be an impractical and unbiblical position which in effect said to the ministers, "You can't manage the church with us, you just minister to us!"

The Office of Overseer. Another Greek term *episkopos* is used and translated "bishop" or "overseer." It occurs a dozen times in the Septuagint, the Greek translation of the Hebrew scriptures, used for various Hebrew words meaning inspector, taskmaster, captain, or president. It was a common word in the Greek world of business and administration. Paul, in writing to the Gentile church at Philippi, preferred to use this more familiar term *episkopos* (overseer) rather than *prosbuteros* (elder) (Phil. 1:1). In his New Testament Greek lexicon, Thayer says an *episkopos* is a man charged with the duty of seeing that the things done by others are done right. As the superintendent of a building project supervises the movement of men and materials on a site, making sure that each part of the project functions with the overall purpose, so the overseers of the church are to supervise and coordinate the various ministries of the church. According to 1 Timothy 3, one of the qualifications for a man being an overseer is that he must first manage his household well. The Bible says, "If a man does not know how to manage his own household, how will he take care of the church of God?" (1 Tim. 3:5). It should also be understood that his authority to manage the church is derived from the Holy Spirit who puts men in the office of overseer (Acts 20:28).

In the book *A Theology of Church Leadership,* the authors identify three models of leadership: (1) the command model, (2) the sharing model, and (3) the servant model, committing themselves to the servant model. While there is good biblical precedent for keeping the servant perspective, there is no reason to conclude, as they do, that being a leader means only being a servant and that servants do not command. Managers of households and churches do command. Hebrews 13:17 says, "Obey them that have the rule over you." Certainly, no home can function properly where the children are in charge of the parents.

The Office of Pastor. The third term to consider is the word *shepherd.* It is used sixteen times in reference to Christ who is "the Good Shepherd" (John 10:11-14), "the Chief Shepherd" (1 Pet. 5:4), and "the Great Shepherd" (Heb. 13:20) of His sheep. The term is also coupled with another in 1 Peter 2:25, where Jesus is described as "the Shepherd and Guardian" of our souls. The Greek word *poimen* denoted protection and care, and the Latin translation of the word is *pastor.* Paul said to the elders at Ephesus that they were to "shepherd the church of God" (Acts 20:28), and Peter wrote his fellow elders to "shepherd the flock of God among you, exercising oversight . . . according to the will of God" (1 Pet. 5:2).

What is the function of a shepherd? First of all, he must *feed* the sheep. Jesus told Peter three times in John 21 that he was to "feed My lambs"; 1 Peter 5:2 says to the elders, "Shepherd the flock"; and the older KJV translation says, "Feed the flock of God." Of course, the reference here is to the Word of God (1 Pet. 2:1). Second, the pastor must *lead* the sheep. According to John 10:3, the shepherd "calls his own sheep by name, and leads them out." Interestingly enough, the word *shepherd* is sometimes used interchangeably with the word *governor* or *ruler* in Scripture. For example, in Matthew 2:6, the prediction regarding the birth of the Lord Jesus in Bethlehem said, "Out of you shall come forth a Ruler, who will shepherd My people Israel." (Another translation uses the word *governor.*) In Acts 7:10, Joseph, the prime minister of Egypt, is referred to as *governor,* and it was his responsibility "to rule" (Gen. 41:38-44). While Jesus Christ is *the* Shepherd, pastors, elders or bishops are undershepherds appointed by Christ to feed and lead people who are His sheep.

THE RESOURCE OF MANAGEMENT GIFTS

The Gift of Leadership. In addition to the offices and functions reviewed, there are three gifts in the New Testament given for the management of the church. The first of these is found in Romans 12:8 and is considered by many commentators to be the gift of leadership. Whereas the King James Version says, ". . . he that ruleth," the *New American Standard Bible* says, ". . . he who leads." One commentator, Lenski, even translates it, ". . . he who manages." The Greek word *proistamenos* originally denoted an influential Roman patron who had clients or followers. Later it came to signify any person of wealth or power who extended himself to help others. The root word in the New Testament means "to stand before," or "to preside over," and is translated "rule" in 1 Timothy 5:17, and "have charge over" in 1 Thessalonians 5:12. Some say this is the man who presides or governs in any position, church or secular. But the context makes it clear that this is a gift given by grace (Rom. 12:6) and is to be exercised accordingly in the body of Christ (Rom. 12:5).

Although a few commentators believe this gift is equivalent to the office of elder, the consensus is that the gift can be distinct from the office. In his commentary, Charles Hodge says,

> It is commonly understood of rulers. Some take this in reference to rulers in general, civil or ecclesiastical; others to church rulers or elders; others especially of the pastor or bishop of the congregation. The objection against this restricted reference to the presiding officer of a church is the introduction of the term in the enumeration of ordinary Christian duties. . . . It is more common, therefore, to understand "proistamenos" of anyone who exercises authority in the church.[8]

Other commentators, like William Barclay, simply refer the term to church leaders in general rather than to the minister in particular. It was Dean Alford who first objected to the idea of official rulership being in view because this gift is mentioned next to last in the list. Another author, Rick Yohn, concludes that a pastor may be in a position of leadership without having the gift of leadership. The reverse is also true.

Peter Wagner, in his book *Your Spiritual Gifts Can Help Your Church Grow,* says the gift of leadership for the minister is an essential prerequisite in church growth. According to Wagner, there are two gifts that are evidenced in pastors of growing churches: the gift of faith and the gift of leadership. "If the gift of faith lets the church growth pastor know where he should go, the gift of leadership lets him know how to get there."[9] Inherent in this gift of leadership is the ability, to one degree or another, to inspire and motivate people to positive action for Christ. While Wagner does allow for the gift of faith to operate at different levels, he fails to draw the same analogy for leadership. I think that there are also different levels of leadership given by God to ministers and others. In regard to the gift of administration, Wagner also says, "I think we can distinguish between the gift of administration and the gift of leadership. A pastor can do without the gifts of administration, but not without the gift of leadership."[10]

The Gift of Administration. The second of these gifts mentioned in 1 Corinthians 12:28 is sometimes called "the gift of administration" (NASB) or "the gift of government" (KJV). While some theologians like Walvoord and other Bible teachers like Criswell want to equate these gifts and use the terms interchangeably, there is good reason to keep them distinct. In his book on *Spiritual Gifts,* Kenneth O. Gangel says he prefers to think of these gifts "as closely related, possibly united in a cluster for some church leaders but not necessarily dependent one upon the other."[11] The root word in the Greek is *kubernesis,* from which we get the English word *cybernetics,* the science of relating the nature of the brain to the governing of the body. In the computer world, it has reference to the planning part of the system. Gangel says, "All of its use in Scripture refers to leadership and administration in some secular enterprise except where Paul impregnates the word with spiritual meaning."[12]

Kittel's *Theological Dictionary of the New Testament* says the Greek word *kubernesis* refers to the ship-owners "hired helmsman." In the New Testament, the word appears in Acts 27:11 as "pilot" (NASB) or "master" (KJV) of the ship. It also appears in both translations of Revelation 18:17 as "shipmaster." The owner of the ship decides where the ship is going and when it should arrive. The helmsman or steersman was responsible to hire the crew and to be the ship administrator. He was to steer the ship and keep it on course. This is the man who knows how to keep the church machine running smoothly. In the small church he might be "the minister of all trades, master of none" pastor who maintains close contact with everything going on. In the larger church, he might be the executive minister, associate pastor, or business administrator. In many churches, he might be president, moderator, or vice-chairman of the church and sometimes the chairman of the church board, elders, or deacons. One pastor who was expected to be chairman of the board was a wonderful pastor but a weak administrator, and his entire board resigned out of frustration. He should have secured another leader to be the chairman.

The Gift of Pastor. The third gift mentioned in Ephesians 4:11 is that of a "pastor" or the "pastor-teacher." Many scholars have made the point that the Greek use of the conjunction *kai* ("and") in the text with no articles preceding the two nouns implies that one cannot be a pastor without also being a teacher—that is, the *kai* functions as a hyphen, combining the two words. It seems apparent from the New Testament that certainly the reverse can be true: one can be a teacher without necessarily being a pastor. According to 1 Corinthians 12:28, God has appointed some teachers in the church, but not all pastors have that gift (1 Cor. 12:29). Another interesting thought is that some consider "preaching" to be the modern expression of the gift of "prophecy," and not all pastors are good preachers. In Paul's letter to Timothy, he discusses elders who should receive double honor, "especially those who work hard at preaching and teaching" (1 Tim. 5:17). Since one of the requirements for the office of the elder-bishop-pastor is that he be "able to teach" (1 Tim. 3:2; Titus 1:9), and part of his responsibility is to "feed the flock of God" (1 Pet. 5:2; John 21:15-17), the two functions appear to be part of the one gift or office. One commentator says that

> while this phrase shows that every pastor ought to be a teacher, putting the former phrase of duty first, it will ever be the case that through native endowment, some ministers are better adapted for the one part of the duty than for the other, though there is no warrant for the total neglect of either.[13]

Of course, teaching is not just a matter of native endowment; it is also a spiritual gift.

As already stated, the Greek word which we translate "pastor" is *poimen,* shepherd. The Eastern shepherd was a watchman, a guard, a guide, a savior, a provider, and a man who personally loved his sheep. The pastor of a local church, then, is ideally supposed to be a shepherd, but sometimes he is not. He may be a good preacher, and preaching is certainly important to his pastoral work. He may be a good organizer, but if he is not maintaining a personal interest in the flock, he may not prove to have a divine gift as a pastor. Kenneth Gangel puts an emphasis on the care of the pastor for the flock when he says, "The gift of pastoral care is beyond the level of teaching it; there is implied a dimension of patience, an attitude of long-suffering not essential to the ministry of teaching."[14] A recent survey has indicated that 40 percent of people who seek professional counseling go first to pastors. While monetary considerations may sometimes be in view, a major consideration is that pastors are assumed to really care for those in need.

Again, Peter Wagner defines this gift as a special ability to make a long-term commitment to minister to a group of believers. This person-centered ministry may effectively encompass groups as small as eight to ten families or congregations as large as fifty to one hundred families. Very few senior ministers of larger churches have the gift of pastor. As they become responsible for larger congregations, they also need to change their style of management and, in the words of church consultant Lyle Schaller, become "ranchers" instead of "shepherds." I know of a missionary who does not have the gift of evangelism and may never be the pastor of a good-sized church. However, he has teamed up with an indigenous evangelist on a mission field and is having a marvelous ministry discipling new believers and forming core groups for new churches. I believe this missionary has a real gift to be a pastor.

It is also important to know that people can have the gift of pastoring without being full-time pastors or ministers. Leslie Flynn says,

> Though everyone divinely called to the office of a pastor will of necessity receive the corresponding gift of pastoring from the Holy Spirit, not everyone who has the gift of pastoring has been called to the office of pastor. You may have the gift of pastoring without being a pastor.[15]

Many churches today are committed to small group ministries, one of which is a Lay Shepherding Program. A lay shepherd, sometimes an elder or a deacon, is appointed over a group often identified in a specified geographical location. The "biggest little church in the world," Paul Cho's church in Seoul, Korea, currently has six hundred thousand members *and* at least ten thousand house churches with "pastors" in charge. In many of the fundamentalist churches of America, the captains of each bus in the bus ministry are called "bus pastors." Sunday school teachers and Bible study leaders may also have this gift. Billy Graham once wrote that the gift of pastor includes "ministers of the gospel and unordained saints in the congregation who have the gifts of counseling, guiding, warning, and guarding of the flock. A number of people have acted as spiritual shepherds in my own life although they were never formally ordained to the ministry."[16]

THE RECOGNITION OF MANAGEMENT TYPES

Given that there are three gifts that may or may not be utilized in the offices of management in the New Testament, how do we recognize the difference between them? How do we know if we have those gifts? In general, spiritual gifts may be discerned by a personal evaluation. Is there a God-given desire to pursue or perfect some of the specific gifts we have discussed? In 1 Corinthians Paul said they should "earnestly desire the greater gifts" (12:31). In addition to love, they were commanded to "desire earnestly spiritual gifts" (1 Cor. 14:1). In 1 Timothy he also said, "It is a trustworthy statement; if any man aspires to the office of overseer, it is fine work he desires to do" (3:1). It is clear from the Scriptures that the Holy Spirit distributes gifts in the church to each one individually, as He wills (1 Cor. 12:11). I also believe that as we delight ourselves in the Lord He will give us the desires of our hearts (Ps. 37:5). As such, He not only invites us to pursue spiritual gifts, He can also inspire us as to which gifts we should pursue. In the discerning and development of these gifts, we can discover our distinctive roles as ministers or managers in the church.

The church, of course, should also substantiate what we sense our gifts to be. Though there are varieties of gifts and ministries, Paul says God works in all as "to each one is given the manisfestation of the Spirit for the common good" (1 Cor. 12:7). In other words, evidence of spiritual gifts will be seen in the lives of others. I was once approached by a man who said he felt called by God to minister in music at our church. Though he did have some musical abilities, we were not led by God to call him to minister there. If our gifts are from God, they will be recognized by spiritual results in the lives of those we minister to.

Other tools may also be utilized to help make an objective evaluation of the spiritual gifts of leadership, administration, and pastoral work that we have discussed. In a spiritual gifts seminar conducted by David Hocking, positive answers to a series of questions are used to affirm the probability of particular gifts in an individual. Hocking identifies these gifts as follows:

> (1) A leader is a disciple-maker who motivates people, (2) an administrator is a decision-maker who manages people, and (3) a pastor is a sermon-maker who ministers to people.[17]

The chart on page 70 describes the characteristics of people possessing these gifts.

Another very useful tool is the Modified Houts Questionaire. This material was originally designed by Richard F. Houts, a professor of Christian education at Ontario Bible College. It was later revised by C. Peter Wagner and includes twenty-five possible gifts. It assumes that some gifts will surface as "dominant" while others will be "subordinate." (See the definitions in the chart on page 71.)

A LEADER
• Enjoys motivating others to various tasks and ministries
• Sets goals and objectives for himself and his ministry
• Is concerned to help others become more effective in their jobs
• Would rather show someone else how to do a task than do it himself
• Has a special concern to train and disciple others to become leaders
• Usually takes the leadership role in a group where none exists
• Has a great sense of joy in leadership positions
• Has an instinctive ability to meet people's needs and goals

AN ADMINISTRATOR
• Is described by others as being able to make decisions easily
• Feels responsible to make decisions on behalf of others
• Feels morally responsible for how he directs and guides others
• Enjoys giving directions and making decisions
• Constantly thinks about decisions needed to direct an organization
• Enjoys being the "final voice" or ultimate authority in a group

A PASTOR
• Enjoys spending time in the study of the Bible
• Wants believers to use their spiritual gifts in the ministry
• Enjoys relationships with people with whom he is not well-acquainted
• Likes working with people and their personal needs
• Works with people in a positive and loving manner
• Would enjoy having the spiritual responsibility for all the spiritual needs of a group of people
• Would rather stay in one place than travel in the ministry

The making of a man of God for ministry and management in the church is a divine production. The inherited characteristics, the time of birth, the background and birth order in a family, the discovery and development of natural abilities and spiritual gifts, and the call and guidance of the Holy Spirit are all a part of the sovereign plan He has for His servants. Consider Moses. Before he ever served the Lord he was "educated in all the learning of the Egyptians, and he was a man of power in words and deeds" (Acts 7:22). He was a scholar (who

LEADERSHIP
is the special ability "to set goals in accordance with God's purposes for the future and to communicate those goals to others in such a way that they voluntarily and harmoniously work together to accomplish these goals for the glory of God.[18] A leader therefore • Has a desire to persuade others to achieve biblical objectives • Knows where he is going and is seeing others follow him • Enjoys leading, inspiring, and motivating others to do the Lord's work • Influences others to accomplish tasks and biblical purposes • Has expert knowledge to edify and influence other believers

ADMINISTRATION
is the special ability "to understand clearly the immediate and long-range goals of a particular unit of the body of Christ and to devise and execute effective plans for the accomplishment of these goals."[19] An administrator • Is able to discern when and to whom delegation should take place • Can organize ideas, people, and resources for a more effective ministry • Can make effective and efficient plans to accomplish group goals • Gives directions to others and makes decisions for them • Enjoys bearing responsibility for organizational success

PASTORING
is the special ability "to assume long term responsibility for the spiritual welfare of a group of believers.[20] A pastor • Enjoys the responsibility for the spiritual well-being of a group • Identifies with people over a long period of time • Has an intimate relationship with those to whom he ministers • Has helped believers in prayer and Bible study • Can restore persons who have wandered from the Christian community

would write the Pentateuch), a statesman (who would direct the affairs of a developing nation), and a soldier (who would lead Israel in unprecedented military victories). He eventually forsook the values of his world for the invisible God he would serve (Heb. 11:27). But even then, in his initial service for God (Ex. 2:11-12), he was too self-reliant. As Henrietta Mears remarked, Moses spent the first forty years of his life learning to be something, the next forty years learning to be nothing, and the last forty years seeing God was everything. And along the way, he learned to be a better manager for God (Ex. 18:18-21), as well as a better man of God.

NOTES

1. Lawrence O. Richards and Clyde Hoeldtke, *A Theology of Church Leadership* (Grand Rapids: Zondervan, 1980), 92.
2. Ted W. Engstrom and Edward Dayton, "Aptitudes and Careers," *Christian Leadership Letter,* October 1985, 1.
3. Peter C. Wagner, *Your Spiritual Gifts Can Help Your Church Grow* (Glendale, Calif.: Regal, 1979), 87.
4. Jerry Falwell and Elmer Towns, *Stepping Out on Faith* (Wheaton, Ill.: Tyndale, 1984), 130.
5. Wagner, *Your Spiritual Gifts,* 87.
6. Billy Graham, *The Holy Spirit* (Waco, Tex.: Word, 1978), 134.
7. Wagner, *Your Spiritual Gifts,* 40
8. Charles Hodge, *A Commentary on the Epistle to the Romans* (Grand Rapids: Eerdmans, 1960), 393.
9. Wagner, *Your Spiritual Gifts,* 162.
10. Ibid., 156.
11. Kenneth O. Gangel, *You and Your Spiritual Gifts* (Chicago: Moody, 1975), 17.
12. Ibid., 15.
13. John Peter Lange, *A Commentary on the Holy Scriptures,* vol. 22, *Ephesians* (Grand Rapids: Zondervan, 1960), 150.
14. Kenneth O. Gangel, "The Gift of Pastoring," *The Standard* (Baptist General Conference), 15 January 1974, 20.
15. Leslie B. Flynn, *Nineteen Gifts of the Spirit* (Wheaton, Ill.: Victor, 1965), 67.
16. Graham, *Holy Spirit,* 145.
17. David Hocking, *Spiritual Gifts Seminar* (Sounds of Grace Ministries, Long Beach, California).
18. C. Peter Wagner, "Modified Houts Questionnaire," in *Spiritual Gifts and Church Growth* (Pasadena, Calif.: Charles E. Fuller Institute of Evangelism and Church Growth, 1981), 12.
19. Ibid.
20. Ibid., 10.

FOUR

SO WHO'S GOING TO BE IN CHARGE?

THE THRONE OF MANAGEMENT

How does the task of ministry relate to the *throne* of management? Of course, the word *throne* immediately triggers one of the most fundamental questions of any organization, including the local church: Who is in charge here? Lyle Schaller says this is one of the most important issues in the church today. To help determine who (or what) most influences the decision-making process, he uses a simple technique. The leadership of a congregation is given a list of "influence factors," and the relative power of each factor is given percentage points by them on a questionnaire. Factors such as the pastor, lay leadership, and tradition are averaged out and positioned on a rating scale. The procedure also reveals that discrepancies may exist (a) between philosophical idealism and practical realism or (b) among the people, leadership group, and the pastor in how they perceive the decision-making process operates. It can also surface a substantial discussion about power basis, power blocs, and power brokerage in the local church.

In recent years we have responded positively or negatively to terms like *black power* and *gray power, flower power,* or *people power*. What about "pastor power"?

73

Part of the answer depends upon the definition of power. Power can be

1. authority to command—a position in an organization
2. force—the use of physical or psychological coercion
3. ability—competence and superior performance
4. influence—the abilities of politics and persuasion
5. empowerment—an attitude of enabling others

The proper use of power by a pastor is an essential ingredient in his management of ministry for church growth. If power is broadly defined as "the capacity to act or to get things done; the ability to execute change," then it is clear that if the pastor has no power, he is not a leader. And everyone agrees that without leadership, churches will not grow.

THE POTENTIAL OF "POWER" FOR THE PASTOR

Across the theological and sociological spectrum, strong pastors with authority in their churches are often singled out as the most effective models for ministry. Peter Wagner's analysis of healthy evangelical churches reveals that dynamic pastoral leadership is "Vital Sign Number One." The following survey of broad-based research demonstrates the point that, in fact, strong leadership is very relevant in a wide cross-section of communities and churches.

• A few years ago, the Association of Theological Schools in the United States and Canada prepared a report entitled *Readiness for Ministry*. Based on a study of forty-seven Protestant, Catholic, Orthodox, and Jewish organizations, it concluded that the "rise and fall of membership apparently depends far more on the strength, clarity, warmth, and enthusiasm of church leadership . . . than on its theological viewpoint."[1] (An interesting parallel to this is the thesis of Dean Kelley that conservative churches grow because of strong demands on their disciples.) The report said it was therefore absolutely necessary to upgrade the quality of professional leadership if the churches were to grow and the expectations of the laity were to be met.

• *The Clergy Job Market* reported that the pastor most in demand was the one who provided strong leadership, made things happen, and was somewhat of an entrepreneur.[2]

• After visiting scores of churches over a four-year period, Ezra Earl Jones and Robert L. Wilson, authors of *What's Ahead for Old First,* described "The Effective Downtown Pastor" as someone who is

1. able to appreciate and relate well to people
2. energetic and hardworking
3. very capable in the art of organization
4. in charge of his church staff and is the only generalist among specialists
5. "inner directed"

He has a strong ego and knows what he wants. Convinced he is right, he will be intent on achieving his goals. He really "runs his own show. He is in charge of the situation, and his staff and membership recognize this and accept it."[3]

• In an independent study of thirty Lutheran congregations in New York, Myron Taylor found the best and most effective pastoral leadership was "benign authoritarian."[4] These pastors had clear progressive goals. They also exhibited a natural love for people.

• In a study of growing American Baptist churches in Oregon, Dr. Camper, who conducted the research, said, "I can't think of a single instance where pastoral leadership was not a key factor, if not *the* key factor in growth."[5] Successful pastors were described as strong and dominant. But they were also people who had a strong capacity for positive interpersonal relationships. Growing churches utilized a one-board system of government with strong decision-making power, but there was also great respect for the pastor who played a major role in determining church policy.

• In a study of 350 British Baptist churches, the particular strengths of ministers were evaluted and prioritized by lay leadership. There was a definite bias in favor of churches growing where administration and leadership were gifts favored over pastoral care and even preaching.[6]

• In December 1977 the Southern Baptists published in *Home Missions* a study of their 425 fastest growing churches. The pastors were characterized as experienced, hardworking men with exceptional skills. Their common denominator was a recognized undisputed leadership. Their top fifteen pastors generally denied being authoritarian, but three-fourths of their lay leadership described them as strong leaders who were accessible and warmly human. Their administrative styles were variously described as "aggressive . . . strong . . . optimistic loving leadership with the emphasis on loving . . . not a dictator . . . enthusiastic . . . dynamic—almost authoritarian."[7] In discussing the basic laws of church growth, *Southern Baptist Journal* says,

> The pastor is the leader of the church and not the servant of the church. The committees and deacons serve the congregation under the leadership of the pastor. The autonomous church exercises its greatest democracy in choosing the proper pastor. Then the members follow the pastor.[8]

• In *America's Fastest Growing Churches,* Elmer Towns concluded that for independent, fundamental

Baptist churches "the difference between a growing church and a stagnant one is pastoral leadership. Gifted men build great churches and average men build average churches."[9] In his later research of principles that help build great churches, he found that administration-leadership was the second most important principle, even more important than evangelism in those churches. While those churches tend to avoid over-organization, there is no question that the shepherds are to lead the sheep; the sheep don't lead the shepherd. As one of those pastors said, "I can show you ten verses teaching the pastoral leadership of the congregation for every one that you can find in Scripture that refers to a committee-led church." In the ministerial management model described by Towns, "charismatic" leadership is best for growing churches.

THE POSITION OF POWER FOR THE PASTOR

Historically, directing the behavior of others has been considered the central function of management. Many years ago, sociologist Max Weber did a classic analysis of authority and said subordinates conform to or obey their leaders because they perceive them to be legitimate; they conclude it is the right thing to do. Weber identified three basic types of legitimacy:

Tradition. This can mean the "divine right" of kings and a monarchical form of government or the infallibility granted the pope in the Roman Catholic Church. It is who they are more than what they do that counts. In the local church, tradition can be embodied in a prominent family or an unwritten set of rules.

Legal-Rational. The source of this legitimacy is in laws and statutes, such as the Constitution of the United States, which defines the "division of powers" in the three branches of our government. Denominational polity books, church constitutions, and Robert's Rules of Order often serve this purpose.

Charisma. People often respond to leadership that expresses their values and goals. Some experts believe these leaders depend a great deal on the needs of others for their influence; these needs are then vicariously satisfied through the leader. It is often the basis for reformation, as with Martin Luther, or for political revolution, as with Gandhi. Church growth pastors often provide that dynamic in otherwise static churches. The power is in the person.[10]

More recently, social psychologists Frend and Raven have analyzed social power as existing in five forms.

1. *Reward power* is when compliance or obedience is rendered by the subordinate to obtain rewards dispensed by the leader.
2. *Coercive power* is exercised when punishments or sanctions are avoided.
3. *Legitimate power* is granted by the organization and is expected.
4. *Expert power* is the "authority of knowledge."
5. *Referent power* causes someone to do something because he admires the leader, wants his approval, or wants to be like him.[11]

Another form of social power advocated today is *shared power.* It might well be said that expert power, referent power, and shared power will best create loyalty and commitment in a voluntary organization, but in the church this does not rule out legitimate power. With this background in mind, we need to analyze the ways by which a pastor may assume a position of power in the local church.

Given by God. One theologian has said that church leaders gain absolute authority because of the absolute character of what they stand for. Pastors aware of a divine call to the ministry often conclude with Paul that their leadership is given to them by God. It's not a matter of presumption; it's a matter of biblical assumption. To what extent this can be assumed will be discussed later. It should also be noted that a desire for leadership is not necessarily unspiritual. The Scripture says, "If a man aspires to the office of overseer, it is a fine work he desires to do" (1 Tim. 3:1).

Captured by Confrontation. Early in my ministry I discovered that some pastors have had to capture their leadership power through confrontation. I heard the story of one young preacher who was called to succeed the beloved pastor of a famous Southern Baptist church. In the young man's second meeting with the board of deacons, a prominent layman strongly opposed "the new pastor on the block." Sensing the inevitable power struggle that would ensue, the pastor turned to the board with a quiet ultimatum: "Either that man goes, or I go!" After decades of fruitful ministry, this eminent preacher has seen his church grow to thousands of members and is respected and loved by his congregation.

Of course, such confrontations can cause a crisis in the church that may be counterproductive to growth. Sometimes people leave and the church is weakened in the process. Sometimes the pastor resigns after a long and bitter battle which degrades both pastor and church. Clergy coups are not always beneficial. I once heard the story of a successful pastor who attended a seminar where strong authoritarian style was advocated. Returning to his church, he adopted a very dominant directive role that soon forced capable staff to resign. It appears, however, that he felt uncomfortable with his new role and its consequences and suddenly resigned to avoid congregational dissent. The overly approach was really not his true style, nor an effective one. But despite the potential negative consequences, confrontation is sometimes necessary to establish a positive pattern of church growth leadership. The following two case studies are public examples of this principle.

In 1959 Marvin G. Rickard was called to be the pastor of a long-established 83-member church in Los Gatos, California. At his second board of elders meeting he had a confrontation with the church chairman. Looking him directly in the eye, the chairman said, "Young man, we have always had a good relationship with our minister. Here is how we have operated. Every Tuesday the minister comes to my house. We go over the events of the week . . . we evaluate. Then we go over what is planned. Do you understand me?" With great difficulty Rickard replied, "I am not going to come to your house every Tuesday or any other day to get permission to do the work of the ministry to which God has called me!"[12] God did "honor his stand," and today the church has over sixty-five hundred members.

Over twenty years ago Arther DeKruyter founded Christ Church in the Chicago suburb of Oak Brook. Early in his ministry, he was informed by a businessman board member that he was a pastoral "hired hand" who worked for the church. The pastor, however, was persuaded that great churches had great administrators. In practice, pastors were to be leaders, goal-setters, organizers, and managers in their ministry. So when some board members wanted to set aside the church constitution's position that the pastor was to be church administrator, he opposed them. They debated the issue and had a showdown. When this pastor's nightmare was over, the dissenting elders had left with a third of the church's families. However, he says, since then "the basic principle has developed in our church and is now bearing fruit. The board makes the policy and the pastor administers the program."[13] The church now has over three thousand members.

Earned by Expectations. In a study of twenty congregations, it was discovered that the most critical issue between clergy and laity was the religious authenticity of the pastor. It was also discovered that it must be established in each new congregational setting. According to *The Management of Ministry,* "The minister's credit as a leader is dependent upon establishing a relationship with the congregation predicated on loyalty and trust. People must give authority to the minister before the ministry is possible."[14] This would require referent power and expert power. Authority is not simply divinely ordained; it must also be *deserved.* As one pastor put it, "A pastor can earn this authority only with love and consistent exercise of prudent judgment, showing ability to lead and making exceptionally good decisions. He will then find the church produces a growing trust in his ministry and in his office as pastor." If it is sometimes gained by confrontation, it must still be maintained by character and competence.

In my first pastorate after seminary, the 150–200 member congregation I was to serve had for some time been considering plans to build a new church. For some reason their plans had never materialized. In my opinion, the site location was questionable (a secondary street in an established residential area). One month after I arrived, a layman in the church suggested another site to me. I was then led to recommend to our building committee that we approach some members in our church about the purchase of some prime land they owned on the other side of town. Up to that time they had been unwilling to sell any of their ten-acre property to developers. However, within one week of our approach, they sold the church four acres at only a thousand dollars per acre! Though they never expected the church to approach them, they quickly concluded God had led them to hold on to the property until "such a time" as this. As I look back on it now, I can not only thank God for His gracious provision, but also for a significant "success" early in my ministry that more quickly validated my leadership with the dear people of that church.

E. L. Becker has observed that even "within religious organizations, the ability of an individual to wield influence is related closely to an embodiment in his own person of the beliefs and values of the group."[15] It has been said of Abraham Lincoln that he was a great leader not because he was clever, decisive, a good political showman, or an astute politician. Rather, his moral and spiritual leadership represented those liberal and humane ideals for which our country stood at the time. Pastors are to prove themselves "examples" to the church (1 Pet. 5:3), and the church is to remember those who lead "considering the result of their conduct" and imitating "their faith" (Heb. 13:7). However, while godly character is prerequisite for the minister's spiritual leadership in a church, it is also true that given competence (gifts) must be commensurate with the management demands of that church. Equally godly men are not necessarily equally competent men in the leadership of a particular local church.

THE PROBLEMS OF POWER FOR THE PASTOR

There are some objections to the "strong pastor" image that should be addressed here.

Lack of Love. Who of us has not heard of strong pastors who were insensitive to people, or churches that were hurting because of harsh and heavy-handed leadership? For example, at a large independent church a missionary was scheduled to speak and be interviewed by the pastor one Sunday night. When asked where he had attended church that morning, the missionary said he had not been to church. (The reason—sickness? car trouble?—was not inquired about.) He was summarily dismissed by the pastor and told he could not preach to the waiting congregation. In another church a former military officer turned pastor was teaching his congregation and others through an extensive tape ministry. But on one tape he could be heard publicly scolding people who had come in late for his lecture. His caustic character came across quite clearly.

Lack of love is a liability for any leader, whether strong or weak. But pastors with a strong hand are not unable to have a soft touch. In fact, evidence abounds that good leadership requires a sensitive spirit. Consider some of the descriptions of strong effective church growth pastors found in the aforementioned research. The "effective downtown pastor" was able to appreciate all kinds of people and relate well to them. The Lutheran church study said effective pastors were "benign [not malignant] authoritarians" who exhibited a natural love for people. The successful American Baptist pastors studied had a strong capacity for good interpersonal relationships. And the top Southern Baptist pastors were described by their people as "accessible and warmly human." One national church growth consultant said that where churches elicit an exceptional response from the community, the pastors speak and act with constituted authority exercised "with gentleness." Years ago, Sherwood Wirt, editor of *Decision* magazine, made a study of eighteen great churches in America. He said in his analysis of the pastors that the prima donna complex was absent from the churches' leadership. A gracious, reciprocal spirit permeated staff relations and filtered through to the congregation.

In 1983 behavioral scientists Morgan W. McCall and Michael M. Lombardo wrote an insightful article in *Psychology Today* entitled "What Makes a Top Executive?" In a study of forty-one executives, two groups were identified. Twenty of them were "arrivers" who made it to the executive suite. The other twenty-one got derailed along the way, reached a plateau in their careers and were fired, or forced to retire early. Interestingly enough, the authors found the two groups were astonishingly alike. All of these executives possessed remarkable strengths along with at least one or more significant weaknesses. The major reason cited for derailment was being insensitive to others. The second major reason was being cold, aloof, or arrogant.

McCall and Lombard wrote that the

> ability—or inability—to understand other people's perspective was the most glaring difference between the arrivers and the derailed. Only 25 percent of the derailed were described as having a special ability with people; among arrivers, the figure was 75 percent.[16]

They described "arrivers" as executives who "had the ability to get along with all types of people. They either possessed or developed the skills required to be outspoken without offending people. They were not seen as charming-but-political or direct-but-tactless, but as direct-and-diplomatic."[17] Certainly the scriptural standard for all pastors is clear: It involves being "above reproach . . . temperate . . . prudent . . . respectable . . . not pugnacious . . . but gentle" (1 Tim. 3:2-3). Authority and love are not mutually exclusive.

Abuse of Authority. Along with the success stories of strong pastors and the recent rise of superchurches, there has also come the criticism that power too often involves an abuse of authority. It was Lord Acton who said, "Power tends to corrupt and absolute power corrupts absolutely." Certainly church history shows that this has applied in the church as well as the secular world. It was the perceived abuse of authority that influenced groups like the Quakers and Brethren to originally dispense with an ordained clergy. The strong (and much abused) authoritarianism of the church and tradition in Roman Catholicism was a major cause of the Protestant Reformation.

Some Protestant churchmen today feel the church growth movement has made heroes of these "oligarchs" (strong leaders) so that many local churches are being run by "a Protestant substitute for the papacy." Ray Stedman says,

> Most church members today unthinkingly accept the pastor as the final authority in both doctrine and practice and as the executive officer of the church. If we Protestants deplore the idea of a pope over the whole church, surely a pope in every church is not better![18]

While I personally do not believe truly evangelical pastors ever assume for themselves a position of authority in doctrine and practice over the Word of God, this perspective on the position of the pastor requires some examination.

I believe God has ordained leadership to have authority—to "have charge over" (1 Thess. 5:12), be "an overseer of" (2 Tim. 3:1), and "rule over" (Heb. 13:17) the local church. (How that leadership power may be shared and structured in a local church will be discussed further in a later chapter.) But the Bible also opposes authoritarianism by that leadership: they are not to "lord it over" (1 Pet. 5:3) the local church. Distinguishing between authority and authoritarianism is critical. A few observations will suffice regarding this abuse of authority.

When persons lead in such a way as to think they are almost infallible, they are operating by what psychologists call "the God Principle." These men either have inflated egos and a real abundance of self-confidence, or they are basically insecure and afraid of failing. This insecurity can make them react in an authoritarian, rather than genuinely authoritative manner. They are driven by fear, not love; by arrogance, not humility. The study "What Makes a Top Executive?" found that derailed men tended to be defensive, not vulnerable. Authoritarian leaders thrive on teaching and telling others what to do, but they themselves are often not teachable. They discourage individual growth, private opinion, and genuine Christian freedom. They not only oppose those who are different but oppress those who dissent, even in matters not specified by Scripture. Fear and intimidation are the tools of the trade. Otherwise strong men can tremble in the grip of some god-like leader, and when these abuses are questioned, the leader believes he is being persecuted for righteousness sake.

Ronald M. Enroth admits that "the touchy issues of authority and submission are far from being fully resolved in evangelical circles."[19] But it is very clear that among some of the cults and even in some evangelical circles there are sad cases of authority being abused. (The shepherd-discipling practice is an example.) It is important to recogznie that there is a difference between an authentic authority based on love and an austere authoritarianism based only on power and control.

Loss of Lay Leadership. Another major objection to the strong pastor is the assumption that he always thrives on dependent people. One Baptist leader says, "Domineering pastors tend to produce weak and overly dependent people, whereas people who learn to follow examples must develop their own inner strength and stability."[20] There is a valid concern here. But is this always a valid criticism for strong church-growth pastors? Some critics seem to assume this. In discussing the vitally needed application of the 2 Timothy 2:2 multiplication model for leaders, they assume that a "pastor-centered" church is always dominated by a really strong pastor, populated by a passive people, and unproductive when it comes to new leaders. On the other hand, a dynamic church is led by a strong pastor who shares the pastoral responsibility and produces other leaders. It is true that the pastor is called by God to equip "the saints, for the work of service, to the building up of the body of Christ" (Eph. 4:12-13). But it is not always true that strong, authoritative pastors do not mobilize and multiply strong lay leadership. Again, a case study serves to illustrate the point.

One successful church growth model for ministry has been the First Baptist Church of Modesto, California. In 1967 Pastor Bill Yaeger arrived, and over the next decade it grew 330 percent and has continued to grow until it now has thirty-five hundred members. Yaeger believes the typical pastor probably exerts too little authority and often shrinks back from aggressive leadership because of a democratic decision-making process in the church. In his new book, *Who's Holding the Umbrella?* he says, "A spiritual leader must be strong, [but] it is Jesus' quiet quality of leadership that we are talking about."[21] He rejects what he calls the "Commander Cody" leader who needs to be in full control of everything and makes all the decisions. But he does not believe that the board of the church is authorized to supervise the pastor's work and lead him around at will.

Yaeger's philosophy of ministry clearly includes the

concept of the "umbrella man" leader as one who "gives himself to the ministry of Christ in such a way that he equips believers and provides abundant opportunities for them to serve."[22] He believes, as some modern management experts do, that leadership power involves "the empowerment of others." In one church-growth research project it was discovered that in many churches 85 percent of available time is given to management, while only 15 percent of time is given for ministry. When Bill Yaeger came he restructured the church with a one-board system, and assumed a strong pastoral position so that the people could devote more time to the church's number one priority: evangelism and discipleship. At one time, the church calculated that their people devoted almost 97 percent of their time to ministry and only 3 percent of their time to management in the affairs of the church. No wonder he subtitled his book "Creating a Climate for Effective Lay Leadership in the Church."

While there may be potential weaknesses in the exercise of strong leadership, the church of Jesus Christ will be weak without authentic strong leaders. In a recent biographical study of corporate leadership in action, the authors of *CEO* concluded that an effective leader is someone who "is able to take charge." In their opinion

a major fault of contemporary theorizing on leadership in an organization is precisely that it does not discuss this issue. It is as if writers were unable to differentiate between being authoritative and being authoritarian and therefore, the appropriate exercise of authority is viewed as being not good managerial behavior. . . . Each of our leaders was clearly in control, both formally and psychologically. None had difficulty taking charge and maintaining that control.[23]

Effective pastors must also know how to take charge according to biblical standards with the love of Christ if their churches are to grow.

NOTES

1. Carnegie Samuel Calian, *Today's Pastor in Tomorrow's World* (New York: Hawthorn, 1977), 8.
2. W. Carrol Jackson and Robert L. William, *Too Many Pastors? The Clergy Job Market* (New York: Pilgrim, 1980), 15.
3. Ezra Earl Jones and Robert L. Wilson, *What's Ahead for Old First* (New York: Harper & Row, 1974), 69.
4. Myron J. Taylor, "Why Congregations Grow: Lutheran Church in America; Upper New York Synod," *Pulpit Digest,* May-June 1978, 24.
5. Mary Anne Forehand, "What Makes Churches Grow?" *The American Baptist* 179 (March 1981), 11f, 35.
6. Paul Beasley-Murray and Alan Wilkinson, *Turning the Tide* (London: British Bible Society, 1981).
7. *Home Missions* (Southern Baptist Convention), December 1977, 21-35.
8. "Basic Laws of Church Growth," *Southern Baptist Journal,* April 1978, 8.
9. Elmer Towns, *America's Fastest Growing Churches* (Nashville: Impact, 1972), 193.
10. Max Weber, *The Theory of Social and Economic Organizations.* ed. Talcott Parsons, trans. Talcott Parsons and A. M. Anderson (New York: Oxford University, 1947).
11. John R. P. Frend and Bertram Raven, "The Basis of Social Power," in *Studies in Social Power,* ed. D. Cartwright (Ann Arbor: University of Michigan, Institute for Social Research, 1959).
12. Marvin G. Rickard, *Let It Grow: Your Church Can Chart a New Course,* (Portland, Ore.: Multnomah, 1984), 22.
13. Arthur H. DeKruyter, "Taking Charge," *Leadership,* Fall 1985. 25.
14. James D. Anderson and Ezra E. Jones, *The Management of Ministry* (New York: Harper & Row, 1978), 90.
15. E. L. Becker, "Church and Power Conflicts," *Christianity and Crisis,* 22 March 1965, 26-36.
16. Morgan W. McCall, Jr., and Michael M. Lombardo, "What Makes a Top Executive," *Psychology Today,* February 1983, 31.
17. Ibid., 30.
18. Ray Stedman, "Should the Pastor Play Pope?" *Moody Monthly,* July-August 1976, 41-44.
19. Ronald M. Enroth, "The Power Abusers," *Eternity,* October 1979, 27.
20. Leland Eliason, "How Much Authority Do Pastors Have?" *Bethel Seminarian,* November 1973, 1.
21. William E. Yaeger, *Who's Holding the Umbrella?* (Nashville: Thomas Nelson, 1984), 55.
22. Ibid., 19.
23. Henry Levinson and Stuart Rosenthal, *CEO: Corporate Leadership in Action* (New York: Basic Books, 1984), 260-261.

SECTION TWO
The Maximization of Ministry:
A Typology of Management

FIVE

AUTOCRAT, BUREAUCRAT, AND OTHER -CRATS:

THE STYLE OF MANAGEMENT

The right pastor in the right church at the right time is often the most important human factor in church growth. However, we need not conclude that any single pastor, even the strong pastor discussed in chapter 4, is the master key to unlock the growth potential of any church, regardless of the circumstances.

One pastor of a strong church ministered in Texas for a few years without much success but then went to a Midwestern state where his church grew from forty-five to over a thousand. Another successful pastor-author came from a different part of the country to a large church in the same state and struggled for success. And still another pastor came from modest success on the East Coast to nationwide fame on the West Coast where his church is now numbered in the thousands. Though good pastors are capable of working well in many different churches, some situations are more suitable for growth under the leadership of the right man appointed by God. Several strategic variables in a church can affect its growth potential, the first of which is the pastor and his particular leadership style in that church.

In response to the strong pastor church growth model advocated by Peter Wagner in *Leading Your Church to Growth,* British author Eddie Gibbs replied, "If that [model] is true, most of us had better start packing our bags now. If such charisma and dynamism is essential for church growth, then it must be said that a large number of churches will never grow. Most of us are not in the star-studded first division of the clergy league."[1] Here in the United States there have been some similar comments that Wagner's view makes second-class citizens out of a number of pastors. Peter Wagner admits that perhaps 95 percent of American pastors will not pastor the superchurches and therefore most will be average pastors of average churches. But, to paraphrase Lincoln, "God must have loved common pastors because He made so many of them." Also, pastors of so-called average churches can become more effective in having their churches grow. The United States Military Academy at West Point believes that leadership can be learned by capable, committed men. The same potential is true for pastors. There is also evidence that shows pastors with different styles of leadership are capable of leading their churches to growth, too. While the evidence is clear that strong pastors most often build strong churches, it is not necessarily true that so-called authoritarian pastors are the only ones who can make churches grow.

For example, black pastors are often stereotyped as strong autocratic leaders. I heard of one black pastor in Atlanta who said quite frankly, "I am a dictator! But I do it in love." He did many things without the approval of his board. As a practitioner, he did whatever needed to be done. He had no office hours but was very receptive to people's needs, so his hours were whatever people needed them to be. His conviction was simple: If he felt in his heart something was right before the Lord, he just went ahead and did it. He was recognized by a

Christian publishing house to be a very successful pastor. On the other hand, in a sample study of black pastors in some Seventh-day Adventist churches, more democratic styles of leadership were found to be most favorable to church growth.

Over a decade ago a study was made of six growing churches in California's San Gabriel Valley. According to the researchers, effective leadership was found in each church.[2] However, the size of these churches, their organizational structures, their situational factors, and the particular leadership styles of the pastors varied. Three of the pastors stressed personal, informal relationships and teamwork, but they also valued bureaucratic ideals like planning and organizational efficiency. Two of the pastors were warm and easygoing men who were labeled laissez-faire leaders. The other pastor was a very forceful active leader, but he delegated a great deal of responsibility to others. None was classified as a typical autocratic leader who stressed rigid controls and unilateral decison-making power, although one of the pastors of the larger churches was a man of strong convictions and possessed a powerful personal charisma in his love for people and the Lord. Different styles of leadership in those respective situations seemed suitable for church growth.

In *The Effective Executive* Peter Drucker disagrees with some other management experts and says there is no single effective personality in leadership. In fact, he once said,

> The effective executives I have seen differ widely in their temperaments and their abilities, in what they do and how they do it, in their personalities, their knowledge, their interests—in fact, in almost everything that distinguishes human beings. All they have in common is the ability to get the right things done.[3]

In *The Chief Executive* Chester Burger says, "How corporations function depends in large measure on the performance of their chief executive officers."[4] In his interviews with fifteen top executives, his subjects ranged from "the corporate autocrat" to "the corporate orchestra conductor," all of whom were successful.

Howard B. Johnson, who became president of his father's nationwide restaurant chain at the age of twenty-six, has seen sales in his company go from $75 million to $450 million a year. He is a "corporate autocrat" and has been described as the operator of a "one-man show." He prefers an informal organizational structure that he can control and wants to make most of the major decisions himself. He says, "We can get instant decision making simply by picking up the phone and calling me. We don't have to go through all kinds of committees. Of course, we do have a very capable group of people who refine *my* raw decisions."[5] More recently, he was asked by his vice-presidents to stop overcontrolling the business. He has since delegated more decision-making responsibility to the field with some good results. However, he is still a strong autocrat in style.

On the other hand, Richard Shinn, president and chief executive officer of the Metropolitan Life Insurance Company, sees his role as the corporate symphony orchestra conductor. In his interview with Burger, he said,

> I must keep remembering that . . . I shouldn't try to be the first violinist or be the first oboe player . . . Chief executives who have been activists—that is, who have been deeply involved with others in the day-to-day operations of the company—find it difficult to stay on the podium where they belong. I know I do.[6]

There is no question in his mind that an executive is someone who wants authority to be in charge. Therefore, he is committed to the participation of others in the decision-making process as an essential ingredient to success. As such, he is more participatory in his style.

Pastors of effective, growing churches have usually demonstrated the following convictions about their own particular leadership style.

1. *They know who they are*. They have come to understand their own personalities, gifts, strengths (and weaknesses) and accept them as given by God to be dedicated and developed in His service. They usually have come to be accepted by their church and leadership team so they can operate from that perspective so long as Christian character and convictions control their style.
2. *They know what to do*. Their priorities and schedules reflect their strengths and styles. They know how to do the right things, not just do things right. Yet they know when to adapt their style to the leadership demands of changing situations. They are sensitive to the needs and expectations of others, but they don't have to become someone else to lead their churches to growth.
3. *They know where they are going*. They have deep biblical convictions, sound scriptural strategies, a vision for the future, and effective church growth methods to get there.

Pastors should study the subject of leadership style, its theory, and the models that have been developed to sharpen their understanding of how leaders lead and how ministers can more effectively manage their churches. Though intuition and experience can give us many insights into our own managerial modus operandi, there are many valuable resources on the subject which can enable the pastor to identify and utilize his personal style spectrum to be more effective in various situations. The following survey of the subject is intended to provide the pastor with some insights into his own personal leadership style, as well as incentives for further study.

CLASSICAL MODELS OF LEADERSHIP STYLE

In order to better understand the subject of leadership style, three preliminary observations should be made.

First of all, *style is primarily understood as being descriptive, not diagnostic.* It often classifies a behavior without necessarily defining the reasons behind it. However, understanding the possible causes as well as characteristics of someone's style may be profitable. Although we might misread someone else's makeup or motivation, self-evaluation should make us more effective. To what should we attribute an authoritative style? At least five causes may be considered.

Psychological Causes. Some classify leadership style as the simple extension of basic personality. One corporate executive says, "There are some people who are born managers. They like to run things rather than watch someone else do it." Even in early childhood, dominant personality characteristics can be demonstrated. Whether it is a result of birth origin or birth order as some suggest, some people do develop what might be called dominant personalities.

Sociological Causes. Some would attribute these characteristics to childhood development in the home. Some psychologists believe that a one-to-one response to role models takes place, so that authoritarian parents tend to breed authoritarian children, and permissive parents breed more permissive children. Other psychologists can cite examples of reactive rather than responsive patterns. If a father was weak and dominated by the mother or was permissive and distant from the son, the son may swing the other way and become a strict parent to the point of harsh authoritarianism.

Cultural Causes. An old-fashioned German home may model a more militant view of authority and submission, while a United States student from the sixties may be persuaded to practice a more permissive point of view.

Theological Causes. Our biblical understanding of scriptural values like submission and obedience can also be determinative. The concept of "chain of command" can guide our conduct.

Ethical Causes. We can also want authority for reasons of pride and selfish power rather than stewardship and service for God. Becoming king of the mountain as a boy or ruler of the world as a man can often have the same root cause as Satan's decision to challenge God's authority.

A second observation I would make is that *style expresses substance (what we actually are) but can sometimes be situational (what we adapt ourselves to be).* Our personality and character may by fairly fixed, but we can choose to be flexible in our behavior. To be effective, a pastor may either have to change his style or his situation—change the way his church will operate or change to another church. For example, blue-collar congregations may like a more autocratic style while white-collar churches want more participation. Small-town, rural, or family-run congregations may want a constitutional democratic decision-making process, while downtown, large, or founder-run congregations may more readily accept strong pastoral leadership and a more centralized form of church government. Even state or regional characteristics may influence the acceptability of a pastor's style. The town meeting mentality of New England and the factory towns of the Midwest are different from the corporate world of downtown Dallas or the creative world of southern California.

Each pastor has what might be called a style spectrum, a range of leadership behavior options from which he can choose. However, every pastor has a predominant, and sometimes predictable, style with which he will normally operate. In addition, he has auxiliary or "back-up" styles he may use in response to certain occasions. Similar to a symphony, a leader will have a major theme and one or more minor themes in his style. Many behavioral psychologists question the extent of how flexible a leader can be, believing there are definite psychological limits. Some even feel it is a serious mistake to teach managers to adopt artificial styles that are very inconsistent with their unique personalities. According to one management author, we should distinguish between leadership style and leadership behavior. He says, "Over a long period of time leadership style represents the consistent leadership pattern of an individual. Leadership behavior, on the other hand, consists of specific acts over a short term that may deviate from the long-term generalized pattern."[7]

The third observation I would make is that *style depends upon your self-perception and your perception of others.* For example, the pastor who has strong attitudes about his own call, commitment, and competence but who views others as less qualified or dedicated may be more authoritarian. He generally operates from what Douglas McGregor calls a "Theory X" view of man: People are passive and dislike work, therefore they need authoritarian approaches, rules, and supervision.[8] Within the church the theological equivalent would be an emphasis on the sinfulness of saints. On the other end of the spectrum, a pastor may have a much lower self-esteem or more modest self-appraisal but strong appreciation for the skills and spirituality of other leaders in the church. He may operate from an overemphasis on what Douglas McGregor calls a "Theory Y" view of man: People like work, and if people are encouraged and given leadership, they will be highly creative and motivated. If the pastor shares a confidence in himself and others on the leadership team, he will most often opt for a participatory or democratic style of leadership. His theological presuppositions will parallel McGregor's "Theory Y" and emphasize the sainthood of sinners saved by grace and given gifts by the Spirit. Because personality types and leadership style are somewhat predictable in pattern, it is important in the process of management to make a careful assessment of one's assumptions in our evaluation of others. Our view of others will influence our leadership style in general, or our leadership behavior in particular.

In regard to style, we rarely find any pure prototypes. Human nature encompasses a broad range of characteristics, and life requires a broad range of choices. Pastors may be classified in one style or another, exhibit one degree of style at one time or another, and demonsrate some characteristics of one style or another. As one American Management Association author says, "There are in reality hundreds of different styles on a continuum with the directive type at one extreme and the free rein type at the other. There are, in fact, many different varieties of any one style."[9] Recent management analysts have developed sophisticated style spectrums that are more perceptive and precise than earlier writers. But generally speaking, leadership styles have been classifed along a continuum of classic models that have been expressed in at least four sets of definitions that pastors should understand.

Some of the commentary given on each of these types includes the following generalizations which may be more of caricatures than of concrete characteristics:

The Autocratic Style (sometimes called the Bureau-

Model 1	Autocratic		Democratic		Laissez-Faire
Model 2	Autocratic Bureaucratic	Benevolent Autocratic	Democratic Participative		Permissive Laissez-Faire
Model 3	Autocratic	Consultative	Participative		Permissive
Model 4	Autocratic	Bureaucratic	Participative	Permissive	Laissez-Faire

cratic Autocrat). This style may include identification of the strong natural leader (SNL) or the minister who wants to run a one-man show. He wants to make most of the decisions unilaterally, exercise tight controls, and delegate little authority to others. He tends to determine policy as well as direct process. There is a strong reliance on authority. The more bureaucratic, the more reference there is to rules and regulations in the organization. The less love, the more dictatorial the description. He might be called "commander clergyman."

The Benevolent Autocratic Style (sometimes called the Paternal Autocrat). This style may include identification of the "father figure" whether it be in Baptist, Pentecostal, Orthodox, or Catholic churches. He knows where he wants to go, but he would rather pull people than push people to go with him. He may lead with a strong hand, but he expresses a soft heart. He cares for people, not just programs and projects. He might be admiringly called "our loving leader."

The Democratic Style (sometimes called the Participatory Style). This style may include identification of the "player-coach" who wants to work with the group. He facilitates decision making by others, tries to build love and loyalty into his relationships, is willing to delegate, and his motto is "Cooperate." While benevolent autocrats may practice the same principles, these pastors major on mutuality and are more patient in the process to bring about consensus. He might be affectionately called "our mutual minister."

102

The Laissez-Faire Style (sometimes called the Permissive Style). This French word means "to leave alone." This style may include identification of the "figurehead" leader who gives little or no direction and dynamic personal involvement to the organization. As a pastor, he either assumes the congregation can run well enough without him or he wants to keep people happy by giving them free rein. It sometimes represents a lack of responsibility, insecurity, or an indecisive position. He might be appropriately called "pastor pushover."

According to *Executive Leadership,* the following delineations may also be made in these definitions:

COMPARISON OF LEADERSHIP STYLES			
Area Of Concern:	Tight Control	Team Approach	Free Rein
Who Does Planning?	Leader	Leader Plus Group	Individuals or Groups
Who Does Problem-Solving?	Leader	Leader Plus Group	Individuals or Groups
Who Makes Decisions?	Leader	Leader Plus Group	Individuals or Groups
What Is Direction of Communications?	Down	Down, Up, And Across	Across
Where Is Responsibility for Achievement Felt?	Leader	Leader Plus Group	Not Felt
Where Does Final Responsibility Actually Lie?	Leader	Leader	Leader
Leader's Confidence In Subordinates	None	High	High
Leader's Rapport with Subordinates	Low	High	Questionable
Amount of Delegation of Authority by Leader	None	Lots	Lots
Crisis Management	Good	Poor	Chaotic
Change Management	Poor		Ineffective

From Mary E. Tranel and Helen Reynolds, *Executive Leadership* (Englewood Cliffs, N.J.: Prentice-Hall, 1981). Used with permission.

CONTINGENCY MODELS OF LEADERSHIP STYLE

For the first half of this century, classical management theory underlying these models made an assumption: The inherent values of style and strategies were universally applicable to all situations. The oldest form of leadership research until then was the search for clusters of traits that could be found in all successful leaders. However, in 1948 a man named Ralph Stogdill reviewed over 124 empirical studies of personal factors associated with leadership and, with few exceptions, found no universals because personal characteristics valued in one group or organizational setting were not equally valued in other settings. By 1974 he had reviewed over five-thousand leadership studies and reported his conclusions in a comprehensive "required reading" for minister-managers entitled *Handbook of Leadership.*[10] Research by then had shifted its focus from trait theories and classical universal leadership models to situational leadership models.

For the last forty years or so, studies have been establishing the thesis that leadership style must be suitable to the situation to be successful. In 1967 Fred Fiedler wrote *A Theory of Leadership Effectiveness,* in which he proposed the contingency model of leadership. He found certain types of workers responded best to democratic leadership, while others responded best to firmer, more autocratic leadership. As such, he concluded that "except perhaps for the unusual case, it is simply not meaningful to speak of an effective leader or an ineffective leader: we can only speak of a leader who tends to be effective in one situation and ineffective in another."[11] For a while, participatory management was considered the most effective leadership style in all situations. As a result of research in the late sixties, many management experts abandoned the participative approach; rather it defined the areas in which participative management is and is not an effective management tool and, even more important, identified the kinds of participative management most effective for different kinds of supervisors in different kinds of situations.[12]

In the late seventies, a study of NFL coaches (including Dallas Cowboys' Tom Landry) concluded that successful coaches are more fluid and adaptable in their leadership behavior than unsuccessful coaches.[13] Even in the eighties, McGregor's classic Theory Y and Theory X have been changed and a new theory proposes both assumptions are correct at different times with different people.

Today, the concept of situational or contingency management has been refined and applied as a basic integrating principle to all areas of management theory. In the late sixties a contingency model called a "life-cycle theory of leadership" was developed by authors Hersey and Blanchard. This model advocates "different strokes for different folks," and Blanchard has said that there is nothing so unequal as the equal treatment of unequals. The maturity level of the group or individual is revealed in independent or dependent responses, active or passive responses, and flexible or rigid behavior. In response to these characteristics, the leader will emphasize task or relationship styles appropriate to the situation. Four basic styles are possible:

1. *Directing:* the leader provides specific instructions and close supervision.
2. *Coaching:* the leader adds to directive behavior an explanation of decisions and solicits participation in the process.

3. *Supporting:* the leader facilitates and supports subordinates toward task accomplishment and shared decision-making responsibility with them.
4. *Delegating:* responsibility for problem solving and decision making is turned over to subordinates.

This model has been more recently described by Paul Hersey as *The Situational Leader,*[14] and Blanchard has popularized the concept in his book *Leadership and the One-Minute Manager.*[15] He has added two factors to help the manager evaluate the maturity of the group or individual. The first factor is competence—the ability or aptitude of the person. The second is commitment—the availability or attitude of the person. The latter is made up of confidence in one's ability and motivation to do the job. The person "ready, willing, and able" is most ideal. The basic concepts of this "situational leadership" model have also been adapted by Norman Shawchuck in some very useful materials entitled *How to Be a More Effective Church Leader.*[16] The basic principles of contingency models are applicable to church life, and a further exploration of situational variables in a church will be explored in a later chapter.

COMPLEMENTARY MODELS OF LEADERSHIP STYLE

In addition to the classic and contingency models surveyed, there are some excellent complementary models that the interested reader should refer to on the comparison chart. An important assumption in these models that I would affirm is that people are born with basic personality potential. Choices in life, the passing of time, and, of course, the grace of God all help determine our development in unique ways. But still it seems we all have basic personality profiles. The apostle Paul is a classic case study. Before his conversion, he was very conscientious and totally committed to his cause—a dominant, driven personality. After his conversion, he was basically the same kind of person, but his purpose and values in life were transformed. Yet he never did become a Barnabas, nor could he.

In these models there seem to be two prototypes used to build a model. The first of these is the ancient theory of four basic temperaments developed by the famous Hippocrates: (1) choleric, (2) sanguine, (3) melancholic, and (4) phlegmatic temperaments. The other is the psychological types first advocated by Carl Jung in 1923. Again, only a brief explanation of these models with some examples can be given to conclude this chapter's survey of style.

Myers-Briggs Model. This model has become the most widely used personality measurement for the nonpsychiatric population and is used in many Christian organizations as well. It assumes that there are orderly reasons for personality differences, and the kind of excellence people can develop is determined by inborn preferences. Adding to the conceptual framework of Jung's theory on personality, it includes other auxiliary processes in four dimensions: (1) ways of perceiving—direct (S—sensing) and indirect (N—intuition), (2) ways of judging by facts (T) or feelings (F), and (3) ways of responding by introversion (I) or extroversion (E), and (4) ways of orientation to reality by judgment (J) or perception (P). One basic type is the NT, the intuitive thinker who is a visionary leader and architect of change who focuses on possibilities. The support system, like an aide with his general, can add two other dimensions. An example would be the ENTJ (extroverted thinker with intuition) or "field marshal" who represents 5 percent of the population. He has a driving urge to lead and take charge, give structure, make plans, and achieve goals. He will usually rise to positions of responsibility and enjoys being an executive.

LaHaye's Temperaments Model. Using Hippocrates'

terms, Tim LaHaye may talk about Sparky Sanguine who is the warm, personal, outgoing type or Rocky Choleric, the more ordinary extrovert who is a hard-driving executive out to change his world. LaHaye is convinced that "humanly speaking, nothing has a more profound influence on your behavior than your inherited temperament."[17] LaHaye feels that too many pastors are reluctant to be strong leaders, but he admitted in an interview that strong leadership is difficult for some pastors because of their basic temperaments. There is no question in his mind that pastors will not be all things to all people in their ministries. (A question I have had in my mind is whether or not there is any connection between a pastor's temperament and his choice of denomination. I think there is.)

Bolton's Social Style/Management Style. This model has four basic types of social style. They are:

1. the driver, who is a control specialist
2. the expressive, who is a social specialist
3. the amiable, who is a supportive specialist
4. the analytical, who is a technical specialist.

An important factor to recognize here in regards to the "strong pastor" model is that a simple classification of a driver style does not adequately express the variation on the theme. In combination with other characteristics a pastor could be (a) a driving analytical, (b) an analytical driver, (c) a driving driver, (d) an amiable driver, (e) an expressive driver, (f) a driving amiable, or (g) a driving expressive. This is to say that there are more precise personality descriptions available in our study of style and church growth pastors than we have thus far utilized.

James David Barber's Presidential Types. He analyzes leadership in terms of performance (active or passive) and attitude (positive or negative). President Kennedy was an active-positive leader with charisma who could inspire people to goal achievement. He said, "Ask not what your country can do for you, ask what you can do for your country." On the other hand, President Nixon was an active-negative leader who wanted the power that went with his position. According to Barber, one can predict a president's performance by understanding his character (developed in childhood), his worldview (developed in adolescence) and his style (developed in early adulthood). His book is a masterpiece worth reading by ministers, and in David McKenna's application of this model, he says, "A pastor's style is a many-splendored thing." God calls all types into the ministry "to make the most of the personality which we have inherited and developed."[18]

James McGregor Burns's Model. Simply stated, Burns says there are two kinds of leaders. A transactional leader is one who primarily seeks to be custodial in his approach; he is maintenance-oriented. A transforming leader is one who primarily seeks to be a change agent in his approach; he is motivation-oriented.

Robert Dale's Minister-Leader Model. This Christian writer uses some of the same basic framework as some other models but most effectively links it with a situational approach matching a minister's style to a congregation's need. His four types are:

1. The catalyst: an effective active-positive minister who, in Elton Trueblood's words, is "a player-coach"
2. The commander: an efficient active-negative minister who provides structure, goals, and motivation for his people and expects them to follow
3. The encourager: an empathetic passive-positive minister who stresses feeling and fellowship
4. The hermit: an exclusivistic, passive-negative minister who believes his primary work is in the study, not with the saints.

In conclusion, I would like to refer to one more model that I was recently introduced to and have found most perceptive and applicable to management for ministers. I took a simple self-assessment test called the Biblical Personal Profile, which concluded my personal behavioral style was that of a developer. This appraisal indicated I am someone who likes to initiate a task without being prodded and go on to develop ideas or programs for others to complete. The appraisal also showed my potential strengths and weaknesses and the style of leadership I would most likely exhibit.

This personal profile model of human behavior identifies four dimensions which can be used to describe fifteen profile patterns. Sometimes called the DISC model, it involves the following features:

1. *Dominance.* Pastors with these tendences want to take charge of their environment to bring about needed change. They will be more highly task-oriented.
2. *Influencing.* These pastors are much more people-oriented and want to bring about change by stimulating and facilitating others to action. They are usually very warm in their relationships and possess good verbal and social skills.
3. *Steadiness.* These pastors tend to major on stability and maintenance of traditions. They are usually loyal, patient, and supportive of others.
4. *Compliance.* These pastors are very conscientious, attentive to detail, and concerned about rules, regulations, and order. They work systematically and are often sensitive and intuitive.

Regarding the variety of styles that may be effective for leaders, Performax has conducted a very relevant study of the personal profiles of forty-five chief execu-

MODELS	TYPE	TYPE	TYPE	TYPE	TYPOL-OGY
1. Myers-Briggs Temperament Types[20]	NT Leader	NF Catalyst	SP Negotiator	SJ Stabilize	16 Types
2. Tim LaHaye Temperaments[21]	Choleric	Sanguine	Melancholy	Phelgmatic	12 Types
3. Bolton's Social Styles[22]	Driver	Expressive	Amiable	Analytical	16 Types
4. James D. Barber Presidential Types[23]	Active Negative	Active Positive	Passive Positive	Passive Negative	4 Types
5. J. McGregor Burns[24]	Transforming		Transactional		2 Types
6. Robert Dale Minister-Leaders[25]	Com-mander	Catalyst	Encourager	Hermit	4 Types
7. DISC Model[26]	Domin-ance	Influencing	Steadiness	Compliance	15 Types

tives.[19] The following conclusions about style are pertinent to pastors:

- The majority of these executives did not feel they possessed the work behavioral style required in their positions.
- Dominance styles were perceived as best by 75 percent of the executives, and influencing styles were seen as best by 25 percent, yet half of them were basically steadiness or compliance types.
- In addition, three-fourths of them were not totally comfortable with their sense of self-identity because they saw their basic styles as inconsistent with the role expectations of others.
- These successful chief executives (1) maximized their strengths and minimized their weaknesses, (2) adapted their styles, as necessary, to their situations,

and (3) developed a positive attitude about themselves which built other's confidence and trust in them.

In summary, I would make three simple suggestions regarding style. First of all, analyze the models I have mentioned to help you assess your own personal style. Second, research some of the material I have surveyed, and, if at all possible, take some of the assessment tests to be more accurate in your analysis. Third, ask how adaptable you can really be and whether you really fit in to the structure of your ministry.

NOTES

1. Eddie Gibbs, *I Believe in Church Growth* (Grand Rapids: Eerdmans, 1981), 358.
2. David William and James Murphy, "Church Growth and Church Health" (D.Min., thesis, Fuller Theological Seminary, 1974), 154.
3. Peter R. Drucker, *The Effective Executive* (New York: Harper & Row, 1967), 21-22.
4. Chester Burger, *The Chief Executive: Realities of Corporate Leadership* (Boston: CBI Publishing Co., 1978), 3.
5. Chester Burger, "The Chief Executive," *TWA Ambassador,* September 1978, 36.
6. Ibid.
7. Howard M. Carlisle, *Situational Management: A Contingency Approach to Leadership* (New York: AMACOM, a division of American Management Associations, 1973), 133.
8. Douglas McGregor, *The Human Side of Enterprise* (New York: McGraw-Hill, 1960).
9. Carlisle, *Situational Management,* 140.
10. Ralph Stogdill, *Handbook of Leadership* (New York: Free, 1974).
11. Quoted in Howard M. Carlisle, *Situational Management,* 125.
12. Robert J. Mockler, "Situation Theory of Management," *Harvard Business Review* 49, May-June 1971, 148.
13. K. Kerin and C. D. Waldo, "NFL Coaches and Motivation Theory," *Michigan State University Business Topics,* Autumn 1978, 15.
14. Paul Hersey, *The Situational Leader* (New York: Warner Books, 1984).
15. Kenneth Blanchard, Patricia Zigrimi, and Dora Zigrimi, *Leadership and the One-Minute Manager* (New York: William Morrow, 1985).
16. Norman Shawchuck, *How to Be a More Effective Church Leader* (Downers Grove, Ill.: Spiritual Growth Resources, 1981).
17. Tim LaHaye, "What's Your Type?" *Spirit,* September-October 1985, 20.
18. David L. McKenna, "A Pastor's Style Is a Many Splendored Thing," *Action* (National Association of Evangelicals), Winter 1978, 22.

19. Eugene S. Kostiuk, "A Study of the Personal Profiles of Chief Executive Officers of Leading Businesses of the State of Hawaii" (Performax Systems International, Minneapolis, Minnesota, 1981).
20. Based on Isabel Briggs and Peter B. Myers, *Gifts Differing* (Palo Alto, Calif.: Consulting Psychologists Press, 1980) and Marilyn Bates and David Keirsey, *Please Understand Me: An Essay on Temperament Styles* (Delmar, Calif.: Promethean Books, 1978).
21. Based on Tim LaHaye, *Spirit-Controlled Temperament* (Wheaton, Ill.: Tyndale House, 1982), *Understanding the Male Temperament* (Old Tappan, N.J.: Fleming H. Revell, 1977), *Transformed Temperaments* (Wheaton, Ill.: Tyndale House, 1971), and *LaHaye Temperament Analysis* (Family Life Seminars, P.O. Box 16000, San Diego, CA 92116).
22. Based on Robert Bolton and Dorothy Grover Bolton, *Social Style/Management Style: Developing Productive Work Relationships* (New York: AMACOM, a division of American Management Association, 1984).
23. James David Barber, *The Presidential Character: Predicting Performance in the White House,* 2nd ed. (Englewood Cliffs, N.J.: Prentice-Hall, 1977).
24. Based on James McGregor Burns, *Leadership* (New York: Harper & Row, Harper Torchbooks, 1978).
25. Based on Robert Dale, *Ministers as Leaders* (Nashville: Broadman, 1984).
26. Based on the work of Bruce W. Jones, certified *Performax* consultant.

113

SIX

THE PROPER
SHAPE OF THE
PYRAMID:

THE STRUCTURE OF MANAGEMENT

In his book *Ministry and Management*, Peter Rudge makes the important observation that in the local church "the nature and extent of the involvement of the minister depends on which theory of ecclesiastical administration he follows."[1] In other words, the acceptable leadership style of a minister is often dependent upon the organizational structure of the ministry he manages. Many management experts have also made similar observations about other organizations: Structure can either define or confine leadership style. In fact, there are three broadly defined variables that can influence style selection suitable to a situation.

The first variable is *followership*. As we have seen in the previous chapter, situational leadership theory requires "different strokes for different folks" in management. A second variable is *task*. Is the task simple or complex, routine or diversified, independent or interdependent? A military unit on patrol in Central America, a research and development team at Honeywell, or a Ford Motor assembly line will each require a different style of leadership. The third variable is *structure*. Form follows function, but the reverse is also true. The roles we assume can modify our behavior.

The importance of this third dimension can be illustrated by a question that often arises regarding organizational leadership problems: Are the problems rooted in the *people* or the *positions* they hold? Another form of the question might be, Do we find a man to fit a job description or build the job around the man? In the history of organizational theory there is an obvious tension between functional and relational concepts of management. The classical school of management adopts a formal view of organization that focuses on hierarchical positions and administrative principles. On the other hand, the human relations school of management advocates an informal view of organization that focuses on people and social relationships. Lyle Schaller makes the observation that professional church staff usually think more in functional terms, while lay people think more in relational terms. Our answers to questions about leadership problems will depend upon our organizational theory. Experience shows that you can sometimes change the person; other times you must change the position. In this chapter we will focus on positions—that is, on the dimension of structure.

A STRUCTURAL MODEL OF CHURCH MANAGEMENT

It has been said that organizations are people, and churches, of all organizations, should stress people and their potential in Christ. However, a case can also be made for changing organizational structure to be more effective in the ministry of the local church. In *Organizational Analysis: A Sociological View,* Charles Perrow says,

> In working with a variety of organizations, it has been my experience that manipulating the structure, analyzing the goals, and grasping the nature of the environment are more practical and efficient ways of dealing with organizational problems than trying to change human behavior directly.[2]

In his opinion, people's attitudes and performance are at least as much shaped by the structure of the organization as by their preexisting perspectives. Whereas some churches may need spiritual revival, some need structural revitalization as well.

The broad definitions of structure vary, and the minister would do well to learn about organizational theory and the models of organizational behavior that have been identified. For example, the authors of *Leaders: Strategies for Taking Charge* say there are three basic styles of "social architecture" that account for 95 percent of all contemporary organizations. In these models there is often a correlation between the classic leadership styles I have identified and the "social architecture" they have identified.

1. *Personalistic* (laissez-faire) organizations are individual-oriented and may be entrepreneurial until they develop into either of the other two styles.
2. *Collegial* (participative) organizations emphasize teamwork and consensus. This pattern is growing in the U.S. as the Japanese management models become better known.
3. *Formalistic* (authoritative) organizations are constructed along classical management lines, and many Fortune 500 companies operate this way.[3]

The role of the leader as a "social architect" is to choose an organization that fits his style, or try to change the organization so that his style will fit.

According to Rudge, there are not three but five major models of organizational management (see diagram). In terms of organizational concept and the function of leadership in those organizations, they may be described as follows:

1. The leader of a Traditional organization is not the initiator of tradition but the maintainer of it.
2. The leader of a Charismatic organization pursues a vision and is able to magnetize the organization to follow him.
3. The leader of a Classical (bureaucratic) organization sits on top of a pyramid structure and provides the initiative and drive to run the system.
4. The leader of a Human Relations (democratic) organization concentrates on face-to-face relationships and tends to be a collector of group consensus.
5. The leader of a Systemic organization monitors the interdependent network of the organizational parts making up the whole.

In his development of a "managerial theology," Rudge explores two important questions that need to be addressed. The first question is, What is the correlation between organizational theory and the doctrine of the church? Stated another way, Can any of these models of organizational behavior be biblically supported in the structures of local churches? According to Paul S. Minear, there are ninety-six biblical images of the church, and some church structures seem to be derived from these. For example, originally at war with the world, the Salvation Army adopted a military model of church management. Some Brethren groups, concerned about the body of Christ, are strong on congregational consensus. More specifically, I shall seek below to answer the question, Does the New Testament

THE THEORY: SYMBOL NAME FOCUS	A TRADITIONAL MAINTAINING A TRADITION	C CHARISMATIC PURSUING AN INTUITION
The organization: Conception	Historical institution	Spontaneous creation
Purpose of design	Preserving *status quo*	Giving effect to intuition
Source of momentum	Within heritage	Dynamism of intuition
Relation of parts Relation to environment	Coherent; stable Attuned to, embedded in, static society	All focused on intuition Rejection of *status quo;* articulates changes
Decision-making process: Main subjects Nature & perception of goals Degree of consciousness Discrete or continuous Mainspring of decision Communication of decision Nature of response	Recurrent items Generally assumed Nonreflective Continuous; recurrent Announcement of custom Transmission of heritage Implicit consent	Critical issues Highly explicit Spontaneous Discrete; unpredictable Proclamation of intuition Magnetic influence Intuitive accord
Leadership: Dominant personality Functions of leader	Elders; wise; sacred Voice of tradition; source of wisdom; nurturer; guardian	Enlightened Prophetic; inspirational
Control process: Main factors	Strength of tradition; little awareness of alternatives	Judgmental character of intuition; potential withdrawal of adherents

From Peter F. Rudge, *Ministry and Management* (New York: Taurstock Publications, 1968), 32-33. Used with permission.

X CLASSICAL RUNNING A MACHINE	Y HUMAN RELATIONS LEADING GROUPS	Z SYSTEMIC ADAPTING A SYSTEM
Mechanistic structure Maximizing efficiency Leadership drive Mechanical linkage Device for managing mass, homogeneous environment	Network of relationships Maximizing happiness Within individuals Fluid; informal Reflection of cultured, democratic society	System; living organism Maximizing relevance In system; external changes Interdependent Attuned to changing and complex environment
Efficient performance Objective; quantitative Conscious; calculated Discrete; rationalized Issue of orders Detailed directives By coercion	Group goals Subjective; emergent Articulation of feelings Continuous; emergent Consensus in groups Shared Participation	Adaptation to change Definitive; unifying Highly conscious Continuous Expert initiative Interpreted by leader Immediate adaptation
Aggressive; domineering Directive; organizing	Sensitive; cultured Permissive; nondirective; creates right atmosphere; draws out	Expert; technician Interprets environment; clarifies goals; monitors change
Specific standards set by top management	Individual sense of responsibility; answer- ability to constituents	Conscientiousness of expert; corrective of goals; threat of nonsurvival

define for us a normative model of management structure for the local church?

The second question is, What is the correspondence between concepts of organizational leadership and the doctrine of the ministry? More specifically, does the New Testament define for us the unique role of the modern-day minister in relationship to his church or board? For example, does a pastor have *voice power* (an ex-officio status), *vote power* (equal rights in decision making), *veto power* (the prerogative to overrule a debatable decision), or even *vicar power* (the right to rule)? Views on this question vary between churches or even within the same church.

One night I returned home from a board meeting where various perspectives on the pastor's position interfered with the decision-making process. At one extreme there were those who, in practice, were saying, "Pastor, where do you want to go? I'll tell you if you can go there!" Someone else called me after the meeting to encourage me and said, in essence, "Pastor, where do you want to go, and I'll help you get there!" A strong divergence of perspective on the pastor can create organizational division no matter what the focus for debate is. To address these specific questions, we need to examine four historical models and then the question of a biblical model of church management. In the process, I shall leave to other historical scholars and church theologians the finer points of debate and discussion.

HISTORICAL MODELS OF CHURCH MANAGEMENT

The Episcopal (Monarchical) Model of Church Management. This form of church government developed historically in the postapostolic period. It finds current expression in the Roman Catholic church, the Greek Orthodox church, the Lutheran church in Sweden, and the Anglican Church of England. Methodists, Lutherans in America, and some other denominations also have modified forms of this model. In its original form, it was a monarchical concentration of power in one bishop over a local church. Later, it developed into the position of a diocesan bishop who presided over a territory of local churches (the diocese). It is based on a doctrine of *apostolic succession* (Catholic) or *historical succession* (Episcopalian).

Writings of the church fathers indicate that some form of monarchical ministry did exist in the second century. According to the early Christian theologian Irenaeus, Polycarp, a disciple of the apostle John, was called the bishop of Smyrna. Clement of Alexandria says that after John returned from the isle of Patmos, he appointed bishops, which some suppose to be apostolic equivalents, thus establishing the doctrine of apostolic succession which eventually led to the Roman Catholic papacy. In A.D. 115, Ignatius is called the bishop of Antioch, and in his seven epistles he insisted that the authority of the single bishop was essential for the church to maintain doctrinal purity. His oft-repeated phrase was "Do nothing without the bishop." Even so, Ignatius never indicated that the bishop's office was divinely decreed, or that it was rooted in the writings that eventually came to be called the New Testament.

In time the bishops of some major cities, notably Rome and Constantinople, came to have precedence over other bishops, and eventually the bishop of Rome came to be seen as supreme head of the church. The churches in Eastern Europe and in Asia never fully accepted this, and by the year 1054 they split from Rome, though they retained the episcopal form of government. (There is no single head of the church in Eastern Orthodoxy as there is in Roman Catholicism.) At the time of the Reformation, the Church of England severed its ties with Catholicism but retained episcopal government and the idea of historic succession.

In the episcopal system, a bishop heads a diocese, a priest heads a local parish, and deacons, or laymen, assist the priests in their work. (This system is modified in the Methodist church and others.)

I would conclude that the episcopal model is not the biblical model. Even Anglican expositor Leon Morris says, "It is plain that this system is not to be found in the New Testament."[4] But we do need to ask at this point, What caused such a transition from what F. F. Bruce calls a first-century college of presbyter-bishops to a second-century practice of single bishops? In seeking an explanation, he says,

> One obvious consideration is that the emergence of a single leader was almost inevitable in the circumstances. Committee rule, in general, is weak unless there is a strong chairman. Quite often the strongest personality will become chairman in any case, and spiritual strength need not be excluded from his qualities. In practice, such a man will become *primus inter pares* (first among equals), and once his position is accepted and perpetuated, before long, he will be regarded, in theory as well as in practice, as *primus* (first) pure and simple.[5]

Centuries after the emergence of a single bishop, other presbyters acted primarily as his administrative council while he fulfilled the functions in worship and preaching.

The Presbyterian (Republican) Model of Church Management. After the Reformation began, John Calvin wrote his brilliant *Institutes* and returned to the New Testament identification of bishops, presbyters, and elders as synonymous designations for the office of leadership in the local church. Despite the fact that most early church fathers had already acknowledged this (even after the episcopal system had become completely established), it was Calvin who established the model now practiced in the Presbyterian and Reformed traditions. According to Calvin, 1 Thessalonians 5:17 describes two classes of elders. "Ruling elders" are lay members of the local church to whom are delegated the responsibilities of government. "Teaching elders" are usually ministers who preside over the "presbytery" meetings but are not allowed "to rule" as other elders do. Deacons handle temporal affairs.

A question must be raised about this exegesis and its effect on ecclesiology. Is the distinction between (a) "teaching elders" and "ruling elders," or (b) "ruling elders" who teach and those who *especially* labor in the Word and doctrine?" Some passages confirm the dual responsibility of all elders. Hebrews 13:7 says, "Remember those who led you, who spoke the word of God to you." In 1 Timothy 3:2, a bishop must be "apt to teach." Philip Schaff says, "These passages forbid our making two distinct classes of presbyters. . . . Such a distinction of ruling elders belonging to the laity and a teaching presbyter . . . cannot be proved at all from the New Testament or church antiquity and presupposes also an opposition of clergy and laity, which did not exist under the same form in the Apostolic period."[6]

A Congregational Model of Church Management. Congregationalism has both Puritan and Baptist roots. During the sixteenth-century reign of Queen Elizabeth, the Church of England rejected Rome, but those who wanted a purer Protestantism also rejected the Anglican system of bishops. Early Puritans like Thomas Cartwright agreed with Calvin and wanted a return to "practical Presbyterianism." The Church of England claimed it was free to choose an episcopal polity because the Bible had no normative pattern. Separatists who favored congregationalism left the Church of England and settled in tolerant Holland. Later they sailed on the *Mayflower* and established free churches in New England. Baptist Churches in the British Isles also more fully developed the principles of congregational polity.

Classical biblical arguments for a congregational church polity include the following considerations: (1) *The congregation is given authority to select its own leaders.* Although appointed by the apostles, the first deacons (Acts 6) were selected by the church. Elders ordained in "every church" (Acts 14:23) through prayer and fasting were selected (the verb is *cheirotineo*—"to choose" or "to elect by raising hands") by that church. Even later, in the document known as the *Didache* or *The Teaching of the Twelve Apostles,* it is stated each church selected its own bishops and deacons. (2) *The congregation is given authority to discipline its own members.* Unreconciled brethren have recourse to "tell the whole church" (Matt. 18:15-20). When believers lapse into moral sin, the whole church is to exercise discipline (1 Cor. 5). And when false teachers arise, the church is to expose them (Rev. 2–3). (3) *The congregation is given authority to exercise its own ministry.* Christians are to fulfill the great commission (Matt. 28:18–20), administrate the ordinances (Acts 2; 1 Cor. 23–24), and build up the body of Christ (Eph. 4:11–14).

Some critics of this model say it is more of a cultural reflection of the Declaration of Independence than the New Testament. However, a decade before the American Revolution, Thomas Jefferson said he considered Baptist church government the only pure form of democracy whose pattern would be the best plan for the American colonies. One Baptist historian said, "The Baptist pattern of congregational policy, which was the logical expression of the preisthood of all believers, was widely received by frontier people who desired in their religious life the strong freedom which they expected in the political and social life."[7] Whatever the cause-effect relationship in the development of democracy, advocates of congregationalism argue there is a biblical pattern for this polity that precedes the establishment of the United States.

In his classic compendium on *Systematic Theology,* Baptist theologian A. H. Strong presents one view of congregational polity: that is an "absolute democracy." Based on supposed scriptural evidence, in practical terms, he says, "Should not the majority rule in a Baptist church? No, not a bare majority, where there are opposing convictions on the part of a large majority. What should rule is the mind of the Spirit. What indicates His mind is the gradual unification of conviction and opinion on the part of the whole body in support of some definite plan, so that the whole church moves together. . . . To put the whole government of the church into the hands of the few is to deprive the membership of the great means of Christian training and progress. Hence, the pastor's duty is to develop the self-government of the church."[8] Lawrence Richards, in *New Face for the Church,* says church decision making should not be by autocratic decree or even by majority vote, but rather by consensus. The pastor and the board are not to be the decision makers for the church, but are to carry out the decisions of the church. "In decision making, the whole body is to be involved."[9]

Many Christians, churches, and denominations cherish a polity which allows member participation. In *Twelve Keys to an Effective Church* the author says one key has to do with decision and structure.

> The effective congregation has a participatory decison-making process. Whenever three things are in place: ownership, openness and a dynamic relationship between the informal and formal areas of participation, the decision-making process is participatory whenever there is a high degree of

ownership, both for the process and the decisions reached.[10]

I would like to make a few observations about congregational polity. First of all, in a group of any significant size, an "absolute democracy" would be an absolute disaster. Unlimited democracy was attempted in the ancient Greek city-states, but it failed. I met a young pastor from New England who had a female "church boss" oppose a decision he and the deacons had made. As a result, she pressured the whole congregation to require their approval on every single issue. Under the guise of democracy, it became minority rule and reverse discrimination against responsible leadership. To require the total participation of all the members in every decision is neither practical nor plausible.

Second, though some might, in principle, subscribe to a total participatory democracy, in practice, most congregational churches have a *representative* democracy. Even writers who advocate congregational polity admit the congregation cannot be involved in *every* decision. It is really, then, a question of how much decision-making power leadership can assume. Having been a Baptist pastor for a number of years, I can recall those business meetings where even the parsonage telephone bills were read for approval. While the classic biblical arguments for congregational polity are valid for the three areas described, it cannot be demonstrated that these principles are mutually exclusive to a selected leadership that has authority to lead the local church.

Third, congregational polity can be counterproductive to church growth. (This is one of the factors that contributes to a plateaued church, a point I will discuss further when I evaluate size.) Peter Wagner, who himself attends a large Congregational church, once went so far as to say, "For growing churches, the congregational form of government is like a millstone around the

126

neck." In churches where the membership may be one or two hundred, it may be reasonably functional. But for larger churches, particularly those over five hundred, it becomes a function retarder unless the administrative system has been streamlined. Larger growing churches tend to have pastors with more autocratic styles who have developed structures that are not tradition-bound with congregational polity.

A Charismatic Model of Church Management. The remarkable growth of twentieth-century superchurches is, in large part, attributable to the free exercise of charismatic leadership. By this I do not mean the exercise of spiritual gifts, but what might be commonly termed the magnetism of a personality to lead others. Although first defined by Max Weber as a characteristic found in political or military leaders, the word *charisma* (i.e., gift of grace) was later applied specifically to Christians by Noah Webster who said, "Charisma is an extraordinary power (personal magic of leadership arousing special popular loyalty or enthusiasm) given a Christian by the Holy Spirit for the good of the church." One of the best expositions of this subject is found in the book on *America's Fastest Growing Churches,* by Elmer Towns. Here are seven selected characteristics of charismatic leadership found in these churches:

1. The pastor establishes the goals or plans for the church. Having the "gift of faith," he has a vision for church growth that will take risks, set attendance goals, and make faith-projections.
2. The pastor becomes the chief administrator. There is a strong tendency for centralization of authority and executive power to adminster the ministry. Unhindered by constitutional requirements for a bureaucratic structure, standing committees are often replaced by ad hoc committees appointed as needed.

3. The pastor exercises direct control over his staff. Whether or not he uses job descriptions, he requires a direct line of accountability and staff loyalty.

4. The pastor may also assume direct responsibility for the financial management of the church. As comptroller, he may sign checks and have authority to spend what is needed with finance committee approval. Since ministry administration and money allocation are natural counterparts in management, the pastor manages both.

5. The pastor in some cases also becomes the Sunday school superintendent, since Sunday school is the chief agency for evangelism in most of these churches.

6. The pastor is often the founder of the church and an entrepreneur.

7. The pastor models aggressive soul-winning, and it is a major theme in the management of the church. Church leaders, staff, and workers are trained in evangelism and expected to participate in visitation and other forms of outreach. For some, every business decision must be evangelistic in its overall effect. One pastor said, "We don't want a lot of activity and committee work out of our men; rather we want spiritual results. Laymen will work ten times as hard to get souls saved as they will to sit on committees or to fulfill Christian busy work."[11] Evangelistic effectivenss is more important than organizational efficiency.

Towns's excellent examination of the pros and cons of charistmatic leadership is particularly relevant in describing the pastor's relationship to the board of Baptist deacons in those churches. Typically, the deacons do not legislate the pastor's ministry but serve with him in an advisory capacity, sometimes giving approval to certain pastoral recommendations. These churches are pastor-led, not controlled by deacons who exercise delegated responsibility and authority. Towns feels deacon-controlled churches are a detriment to charismatic churches and church growth. He says, "If the second generation of the BBF (Baptist Bible Fellowship) allows deacons to control their churches rather than remaining pastor-led, the movement will be curtailed in growth, especially in evangelistic outreach."[12] Pastors should exercise stronger leadership than the average church structure will allow: they should not abdicate their role to a board of deacons. However, he admits, "Most pastors in America will follow the traditional leadership model as they are not personally equipped to be charismatic leaders."[13]

A BIBLICAL MODEL OF CHURCH MANAGEMENT

People disagree on whether or not the Bible provides a pure model for church management. Some propose a *fixed* pattern—one universal model for all time and every place. Some say the pattern is eldership rule; some say episcopacy; others say congregationalism. Some propose a *flexible* pattern—freedom to develop structure. Michael Harper, an Anglican, says we cannot freeze the first-century church model for all time. Gene Getz, who advocates multiple-eldership rule (as opposed to one-man rule), says, "It is impossible to derive specific patterns and structures from the New Testament. It seems . . . the Holy Spirit planned His ambiguity."[14] From a purely pragmatic perspective, students of Latin American church growth say it isn't so much the *form* of church government that determines effective churches, it is the *leadership* of those who make the decisions.

I propose a *foundational* pattern. There is a basic biblical model to build the church on, but we can add to that appropriate styles and structures as needed for its growth. As indicated, I believe the classic concepts of a congregational church polity are correct but incomplete. In that well-defined context, there is also a biblical eldership that includes (1) maturity ("blameless"), (2) masculinity ("husband of one wife"), (3) ministry ("feed the church"), and (4) management ("take the oversight thereof") (1 Tim. 3; 1 Pet. 5). Many advocates of eldership also include some form of (5) mutuality, a pluralism and sometimes equality of elders. With the exception of a generic reference to a single bishop or overseer (1 Tim. 3), other references to overseers are plural (1 Tim. 4:4; 5:17). And there can be wisdom and safety in a multitude of counselors (Prov. 11:14; 15:22). What, then, is the biblical role of the modern minister? Is he subordinate to, equal to, or above the other elders on the board?

If the pastor is simply subordinate (not *submissive*) to the board, it may seriously limit church growth. For example, in a 1975 study of Church of Christ pastors who left the ministry, 60 percent of them said unsatisfactory relationships with the board of elders was the chief problem. In the opinion of one denominational leader, "The authoritarian role assumed by the elders to hire and fire ministers is the root problem."[15] Another denominational leader says there also seems to be a consensus among church growth analysts that a major factor for nongrowth in the Church of Christ is the lack of pastoral leadership. He says, "Just look around and see which churches are growing. . . . In a growing congregation you will find godly elders who are willing to let the preacher become the leader God intended him to be."[16]

Certainly the biblical model of eldership in principle authorizes at least an equal status for the pastor with his board. Although there may be no real relationship between this structure and church growth success, many contemporary churches feel equal eldership is *the* biblical model because it has proven effective in their own ministries. Whether or not the biblical model may allow the pastor any special organizational status requires a brief review of several arguments I would favorably advance on the subject.

A Biblical Pattern (city or church?). In the Bible, it is clear that elders were appointed "in every church" (Acts 14:33) and "in every city" (1 Thess. 2:14). The local churches of the New Testament were, in fact, the church of the city as in Philippi (Phil. 1:1), Thessalonica (1 Thess. 2:14), some major cities in Asia Minor (Rev. 2–3), and elsewhere. What is not clear is an organizational equivalency for today. They had no buildiings, budgets, programs per se, or personnel assignments. A purely fixed model would require a plurality of elders for one church per city unless we concede that there were elders for the house churches in that city.

A Biblical Precedent (men or committee?). When God wants a work to be done, He first seeks a man like Moses or Nehemiah, not a committee. A plaque in an office said, "God so loved the world, He didn't send a committee." Certainly there is a place for ministry teams, but in Acts 16 Paul received the vision for ministry in Macedonia; then his team responded to it. God's Hall of Fame in Hebrews 11 does not list a committee. In the list of apostles, the Gospels always have the names of Peter, Philip, and James at the head of the sublists. And obviously, Peter is the group spokesman. No book in the Bible was ever written by a committee.

A Biblical Picture (angels or elders?). Most Catholic and Episcopal expositors see the angels in Revelation 2–3 as the biblical foundation for the later development of monarchical episcopacy. Some say they are church clerks similar to the deputies in Jewish synagogues or figurative personifications of the church. Some evangelicals say they are not human messengers but heavenly *angeloi*, since the word is always used that way in the Book of Revelation and nowhere else refers to elders or bishops. Two problems arise with this point of view. (1) Unlike Israel (Dan. 9), churches are not known to have heavenly guardian angels, and (2) angels don't repent (Rev. 2). Admittedly, this is a difficult passage, but most interpreters in church history say these angels are the representative bishops (overseers) of these churches. Phillip Schaff says, "The term is chosen, therefore, to remind these rulers of their divine mission (e.g., the priest in Malachi 2:7, the prophet in Malachi 3:2, and Haggai, "the Lord's angel," in Isaiah 42:19).[17] In either interpretation, a single leader is in view. (An alternative view is that the "angels" are personifications of the seven churches.)

A Biblical Principle (gifts or grace?). While grace gives equal spiritual status before God, not all believers have equal gifts for service. Even though all elders have the responsibility to rule (1 Tim. 5:17), is it not possible that only some, or one, have the speical ability to rule? In some equal-eldership churches, there is often a de facto leadership—some elder emerges as the top leader. In some cases, the pastor is the leader. Carl George says a pastor

> simply cannot abdicate leadership in the process of sharing it. The apostolically gifted person still has to be the leader among leaders, or else the ministry goes nowhere. This is one of the issues where I disagree with some advocates of multiple eldership. They are afraid of the abuses possible in a hierarchy, and so they want to imagine there is no gift of leadership.[18]

A Biblical Purpose (ministry or management?). Some advocates of equal eldership argue it is primarily needed for mutual ministry. However, it can also be argued that all the membership in the body of Christ are gifted for mutual ministry (1 Cor. 12), and eldership is called to the management of that ministry (Eph. 4:11-16). From a pragmatic point of view, many churches have strong, charismatic pastors who are very effective in evangelism and church growth. If the biblical purpose is being fulfilled, how important is a "pure" pattern of plural leadership? A friend of mine who leads the home missions department of a large evangelical denomination once told me it is often the so-called maverick minister who leads his church to grow.

If we reduce *all* leadership roles in the church to pure plurality, don't we structurally displace a number of strong, gifted leaders? When structures are too stifling, those leaders will be attracted to parachurch organizations or will start their own churches. Chuck Smith left a church to start Calvary Chapel in Costa Mesa, California, because his board of directors wanted him to carry out their plans. Being accountable to the Lord alone, as president of his church corporation, his church has grown to more than thirty-thousand members.

A few years ago, when a pastor friend instituted equal eldership in his church, I asked an elder if the pastor did, in fact, function as one who was just equal to other board members. His answer was similar to George Orwell's statement that all are equal, but some are *more equal* than others. Many would prefer to call the position of pastor *primus inter pares* (the first among equals). More modest ministers will admit that the pastor will always be the first among equals, but they prefer to stress *equal* rather than *first.* As in the early church, the position of the pastor may also become *primus,* as is the case in some churches today.

Peter Wagner says many growing churches have strong pastors and single board systems. If a minister feels his church management model is neither biblical nor effective for church growth, there are some simple steps he should consider to change the ecclesiological structure or social architecture of his church (unless, of course, the structure is set in denominational cement).

1. *Pray* that God will give him a clear, biblically defensible position and the wisdom and ability necessary to make structural change.
2. *Plan* an appropriate strategy to present his position to the leadership of the church. Retreats, Bible studies, reference books, discussions, and even sermon series may lead to major change.
3. *Persist* in his conviction until God either changes the structure or the situation. Also, remember that the size and situation of the church may also make a difference in the total structure that is needed.

NOTES

1. Peter F. Rudge, *Ministry and Management: The Study of Ecclesiastical Administration* (London: Hicks Smith & Sons, Tavistock Publications, 1968),119.
2. Charles Perrow, *Organizational Analysis: A Sociological View* (Monterey, Calif.: Brooks/Cole Publishing Co., 1970), vii.
3. Warren Bennis and Burt Nanus, *Leaders: The Strategies for Taking Charge* (New York: Harper & Row, 1985), 133.
4. Leon Morris, *Ministers of God* (London: Inter-Varsity, 1964), 93-94.
5. F. F. Bruce, *The Spreading Flame* (Grand Rapids: Eerdmans, 1961), 206.
6. Philip Schaff, *History of the Apostolic Church* (New York: Charles Scribner, 1868), 529.
7. Robert G. Torbet, *A History of Baptists* (Philadelphia: Judson, 1950), 478.
8. Augustus H. Strong, *Systematic Theology* (New York: Fleming H. Revell, 1907), 905.
9. Lawrence D. Richards, *A New Face for the Church* (Grand Rapids: Zondervan, 1970), 129.
10. Kennon L. Callahan, *Twelve Keys to an Effective Church* (San Francisco: Harper & Row, 1983), 55-56.
11. Elmer Towns, *America's Fastest Growing Churches* (Nashville: Impact, 1972), 51.

12. Ibid., 192.
13. Ibid., 209.
14. Getz. *Sharpening the Focus,* 162
15. Wayman D. Miller, *The Role of the Elders in the New Testament Church* (Tulsa: Plaza, 1980), 79.
16. D. Dwayne Davenport, "The Bible Says Grow: Church Growth Guidelines for the Church of Christ" (Church Growth/Evangelism Seminar, Williamson, W.V., 1978), 33.
17. Schaff, *History of the Apostolic Church,* 538.
18. Carl George, "Behind the Firehouse Syndrome," *Leadership,* Winter 1985. 20.

SEVEN

THE DYNAMICS OF BIG AND NOT SO BIG:

SIZE AND MANAGEMENT

Understanding the different dynamics of small and large churches is essential for effective church growth management. The differences are not just measured in terms of statistical size. They can be measured in other dimensions as well. In describing "What Good Managers Know," Ted Engstrom says, "What may be adequate management for a small organization may not suffice for the larger one. The complexity of organizations grows geometrically with their size, and the skill and breadth of knowledge required by managers of large organizations of necessity must be broad."[1]

I have certainly found this to be true in church life. In addition to five years of ministry to many churches as a denominational secretary of evangelism and church growth, the Lord has given me a broad range of experience as student pastor of a *small* church (20–25 members), senior pastor of a *medium-sized* church (150–275 members), senior pastor of a *large* church (500–600 members), and associate pastor of a *super* church (1,200–1,300 members). In the process, I have discovered at least three major dimensions of management that may be particularly relevant to size, which will be discussed in this chapter. In order to understand some of the dynamics of different-sized churches, some preliminary questions are appropriate to introduce the subject.

First of all, what are some of the definitions of small and large churches? Though the definitions of a small church run as high as 300 members, it is more typical to define them as having a maximum of 75 to 100 members. If we define "small" in terms of *membership,* then about half the churches in America seem to be about 75 to 100 members, or less. If we define "small" in terms of *worship attendance*, then about half the churches in America seem to have less than 75 worshipers in church on Sunday. Mainline churches with more liberal membership standards tend to be larger than conservative churches, though conservative churches will be growing in comparison to others. Though membership standards and assimilation processes will vary in churches, attendance is generally less than membership.

Are there discernible differences between small and large churches? The basic answer is yes. Though there are similarities, small is not just a mini-model of a large church.

Consider at least eight differences that can be observed:

- *Preaching* may be just acceptable in a small church; it is often exceptional in a large church.
- *Pastoral care* is a personal touch in a small church; it is a professional touch in a large church.
- *Pastoral staff* may be one generalist in a small church; it means additional specialists in a large church.
- *Perception* of church life is primarily relational in a small church; it is functional in a large church.

137

gram development is simplified in a small church; it is diversified in a large church.

- *Personalization* of people supports their identity in a small church, their anonymity in a large church.
- *Participation* of members is immediate and direct in a small church; it is intermediate and indirect in a large church.
- *Potential* is focused on the church in a small church, on the community in a large church.

In 1980 Lyle Schaller presented his perspective on a percentage distribution of various size churches and their common characteristics. Based on his book, *The Multiple Staff and the Larger Church,*[2] the following diagram provides a simple frame of reference for seven sizes of churches:

NUMBER	WORSHIP ATTENDANCE	SIZE	LEADERSHIP	COMMON CHARACTER-ISTICS
25%	40	mini-sized	lay leaders	overgrown small group
25%	50–100	small-sized	shared leadership	comfortable relationships
25%	100–175	middle-sized	pastor-shepherd	optimum size of cost effectiveness
10%	175–225	awkward-sized	multiple staff	self-image of "big" family
4%	225–450	large-sized	multiple staff	need change in decision-making process
1%	700 plus	super-sized	strong pastor	corporate structures

Based on Lyle Schaller, *The Multiple Staff and the Larger Church* Nashville: Abingdon, 1981).

Who should win the debate as to whether small or large churches are best? Here we have to know what is "best" for whom and in what situation. Some would argue that little churches are more effective in evangelism when you compare the ratio of existing members to newly evangelized members each year.

In 1976 a Southern Baptist study concluded that newer, smaller churches were the most effective evangelistic organizations in their denomination. Using a "baptism rate" (the number of baptisms per resident members each year), they discovered the new small churches, which accounted for 10 percent of their total baptisms, had a rate of 11:4, while older, larger churches had a rate of 3:7, "making them the least effective evangelistic organizations in the SBC."[3]

On the other hand, a 1977 Presbyterian church study concluded that "there does not appear to be a certain size church that is particularly likely to receive a high percentage of new members."[4] In that case study, the annual percentage of new members received was 9.7 percent for churches under 200, 7.8 percent for churches 200–499, 8.9 percent for churches 500–1,000, and 9.8 percent for churches over 1,000. (However, the report does not say how many new members were the result of evangelism as opposed to transfer growth.) While it is true that larger churches have to work harder to keep up the ratio, it is also true that thousands of smaller churches have not worked any harder or smarter to do the same. I have to wonder how effective it is for one denomination I observed that had 75 churches in a single California city of 100,000 people.

The debate over size often reflects the subjective values of people. Their background, personality type, or church experience affects their preference. Some people like a small church for social reasons: the intimacy factor, the close communication network, the control options, etc. Others like a big church for its sense of achievement, professionalism, and diversified services. What is most important in the debate is not just what size it is, but whether the size of the church is appropriate for its situation. Is the church the size it can be? Is it a growing church? Success isn't how far you get, but the distance you travel from where you started. The debate should not be in either/or terms. Every church, regardless of size, should seek to develop its ministry and expand its membership.

Are there organizational restrictions in the growth of small and large churches? Evidence is in the affirmative. In his insightful book *The Pyramid Principle,* David Womack says, "Many churches tend to level off at certain stages of growth and there remain unless they recognize their problems and restructure for the next stage of development."[5] Elmer Towns's *America's Fastest Growing Churches* also concludes that "there are churches which reach a certain level of growth and proceed no further. Although these levels of growth are not numerically precise, there appear to be some similarities between the organizational structure of the churches that develop the problem."[6]

Authors like Womack who have tried to identify these "church growth ceilings" generally refer to ten church sizes that tend to plateau: (1) 50, (2) 75–90, (3) 120–125, (4) 175–200, (5) 250–275, (6) 400, (7) 600, (8) 800, (9) 1,000, and (10) 1,200–1,400. Some church growth ceilings seem to be more difficult to break through than others. For example, half of America's churches may be 75 in size because the people do not want to move out of the comfort zone of a large primary group. Womack also says, "If the church remains at this level for very long, two or three families will dominate the church and protect its position of influence for their own clan members."[7] Pioneers who have founded the ministry, married into it, or inherited it resist later settlers who threaten their territorial rights. The primary problem is what I would call *social management.*

The next major church growth ceiling is about 200, and approximately 80 to 85 percent of all churches are under this size. It has been common among church growth advisors to point out the need for a pastor at this size church to change his style from being a "shepherd" to becoming a "rancher." At this point it is critical that laymen or staff be deployed in leadership and service. Another important ceiling is about 400–450. Lyle Schaller says the pastor at this size church needs to be "a well-organized and personally attractive individual . . . who can effectively work with a large staff required to care for such a big operation."[8] At either stage a primary problem is what I would call *skills management*.

As churches grow larger it also becomes apparent that organization must change. When a church reaches the major church growth ceiling of 1,200–1,400, Charles Mylander says there is "a whole new set of problems—a church moves from a simple organization to a complex organization. The need develops for sophisticated managerial leadership at the top with effective business administration throughout the ministry."[9] The primary problem here is what I would call *structural management*.

It is not easy to break through church growth ceilings to new heights of growth. Some churches simply accept their status quo plateau and do not acknowledge that there is a problem. Other churches remain too long on a plateau, making the necessary changes much more difficult. Other churches recognize the problem but do not sufficiently explore the solutions that may be available. To break through a church growth ceiling will require at least four essential ingredients for effective change:

1. A strong but suitable style of pastoral leadership
2. A significant power thrust which either pushes or pulls the church to change
3. A leadership in the congregation that is flexible and not tradition-bound
4. Exploration of the following dimensions of manage-

ment that may make a difference in the size of the church.

While the following discussion may not be comprehensive, it will provide some guidelines for ministers trying to break through ceilings to church growth.

THE SOCIAL MANAGEMENT OF GROWING CHURCHES

One of the chief characteristics necessary for a healthy, growing church is love. Its functional form is often called "fellowship," and while its essence is spiritual, it is expressed in the social dimension of life. The Institute for American Church Growth has concluded that there is "a close correlation between growing churches and loving churches—regardless of the size. There is increasing evidence to indicate that the fundamental principle of church growth . . . is love!"[10] In their survey of 7,500 people in 36 different denominations, they found the LCQ ("love-care quotient") of churches and denominations was always higher where there was a positive growth pattern. As churches grow larger, however, the love felt from the pastor or other people usually declines. As such, ministers must learn the appropriate skills of social management if they want their churches to grow. People today need and want a relational experience of Christian faith.

Critical to our understanding of this dimension is the social science definition of primary and secondary groups. Primary groups are characterized by

1. intimate, face-to-face relationships
2. a common "roots" system through families, the community, or ethnic heritage
3. a social identification with each other as "we" (versus "they")

142

4. a strong communication network of no more than sixty adults
5. a satisfied preoccupation with themselves and the maintenance of their value system
6. a tradition-bound perspective that is resistant to change
7. an inability or unwillingness to assimilate new members or leaders
8. a lack of significant goals or futuristic orientation

Small churches, as well as some groups in large churches (e.g., Sunday school classes), often function as primary groups.

In his astute analysis of small churches, Carl Dudley says,

> The basic obstacle to growth life is the satisfaction of the present church membership. The small church is already the right size for everyone to know, or know about, everyone else. This intimacy is not an accident. The essential character of the small church is this capacity to care about people personally. The small church cannot grow in membership size without giving up its most precious appeal, its intimacy.[11]

Large churches are often criticized for their lack of intimacy. Dr. G. Campbell Morgan once said no church ought to be so large that everyone couldn't know everybody else in it. He felt his own church of over a thousand members was too large to meet this standard. A common complaint of large church dropouts is that they feel lost in the crowd or no one really cares about them. Outsiders' entrance into the intimacy zone of small churches, and groups within large churches, is clearly a problem.

Solutions to these social management problems may be methodological or motivational. Methodological solutions may be twofold, the first of which is to subdivide the church for growth through group expansion. A broad range of options is available in two categories:

Sunday School Classes: Studies show that adults actually attend classes more for social relationships than educational opportunities. Some experiments with the addition of new classes or the division of existing classes show that in the latter case attendance in two new classes is likely to be larger than the attendance of the original class. By choosing to "divide and multiply" classes that reach a certain size, the Southern Baptists and others have enhanced their growth through a strong Sunday school program. Multiplication of other groups within the church can also contribute to growth.

Community Growth Groups, Etc.: Some churches have used various decentralized models to multiply their ministries to people. Some use the format of "growth groups" that can include prayer, Bible study, Scripture memorization, and even group evangelism, or they may develop "circles of concern" where a small group of families cares for one another in spiritual and social functions suitable to that group. Some larger churches with regional ministries have developed "house churches." The "Biggest Little Church in the World" is in Seoul, Korea, where Pastor Paul Cho has six hundred thousand members in over ten thousand house churches.

Other churches have decentralized their prayer meetings. Stuart Briscoe's church in Wisconsin doubled its Wednesday night attendance the first year of operation. It is interesting to note that a study of British Baptist churches found prayer cells were more likely to produce growth than simple Bible study groups. On the whole, that study concluded that "churches which were growing . . . revealed that more than two-thirds of them had at least a quarter of their activity in cell groups. . . . A church that was not growing was less likely to have a good proportion of cell activity."[12] The second major methodological solution is to split the church for growth through church extension.

Motivational solutions to these problems vary, but one approach by some small church advocates is to simply affirm its social strength regardless of its statistical success. Where church growth potential is severely limited, this may be acceptable. But institutional self-interest in the social dimension of the church is no substitute for spiritual expansion in the growth of the church, no matter what its size. A biblically balanced church expresses Christ's love for others outside of Christ as well as for "each other" in Christ. To this end, the minister must spiritually motivate as well as mobilize his church for growth. How to do this is a supreme challenge for the minister-manager.

THE SKILLS MANAGEMENT OF GROWING CHURCHES

According to a regional director for the Small Business Administration, 90 percent of small businesses fail because of incompetent management skills rather than inadequate money supplies. These small business entrepreneurs may fail for three major reasons: (1) failure to provide adequate administration to conserve growth, (2) failure to develop personnel to insure growth, and (3) failure to recognize or anticipate problems that can restrict growth. In an article entitled "Why Small Businesses Fail," two business professionals identify some other problems that seem applicable to effective church growth management.

The Problem of Delegation. "The small businessman cannot succeed unless he learns to develop good assistants and delegate authority and responsibility to

...."[13] While it may seem more efficient to do things rather than to delegate, in the long run it is more expensive and less effective. An example of this in a church might be the response of a founding pastor of a growing ministry who works harder rather than smarter to manage it. Behind the scenes he might be threatened by competent laymen and the loss of direct control. I know of an exceptional pastor whose church grew beyond four-hundred members, but on one occasion, he assumed responsibility for organizing the details of a Sunday school banquet, including the place settings.

The Problem of Concentration. The purpose of the business must be clearly understood by the manager and organization to survive. It must evaluate its product or service and identify its functional dynamics. A corollary to this is the tendency for the manager to do the things he likes to the detriment of other things that need to be done. He must not only be sure things are done right, he must do the right things.

The Problem of Graduation. When a business grows, the owner has to grow with it. "The entrepreneur is frequently an individual with high technical skills but less developed managerial skills. As the business grows, those managerial skills become more important—even vital."[14] As the manager becomes responsible for a larger organization, collective wisdom says there are at least five shifts in the skills or style required:

1. The manager moves from being a specialist to being a generalist whose major operational speciality is management.
2. The manager moves from being a doer or activist to being a delegator and analyst.
3. The manager moves from being a close supervisor of

the workers to being a general supervisor of the work.

4. The manager moves from being involved with procedures to being involved with planning and policy.

5. The manager moves from being involved in direct technical work to being engaged in more conceptual work.

At every level of the organization, the appropriate human skills (i.e., social management) are required, no matter what the size. As a manager assumes responsibility for a larger size organization, he must practice a change in skills management to be effective.

Various models have been suggested to help us understand the shift in skills required in growing churches. When John Wimber was director of the Fuller Department of Church Growth, he introduced a model which emphasized the managerial role. He identified seven major levels of industrial management which correspond to the management skills of pastors in various size churches. They were (1) chairman of the board, (2) executive management, (3) middle management, (4) supervisory management, (5) foreman, (6) leadman, and (7) the work force. The average pastor functions with leadman or foreman skills in churches with seventy-five or more members. This level of supervisory skills is often called first-line management, as distinct from middle management or top management. Wimber believes that church growth could double if pastors could develop management skills at least one level beyond their present capacity.

Eddie Gibbs has elaborated on this model with some appropriate descriptions for the British scene. For example, the pastor of a church up to 65 members operates like a foreman or a charge hand who is available for personal involvement in every task which comes to hand. He is the ministerial "jack-of-all-trades." The pastor of a church up to 150 members operates like a supervisor who is directly involved with all the people and programs of the church. Middle management represents churches from 150–450 in size, where the pastor "must avoid getting over-involved in the detailed execution and allowing all the decision making to float up the organizational structure."[15] When you get to churches over 1,000, Gibbs says, the pastor should function like the chairman of the board.

Other models emphasize the ministerial role. A lesser-known version of this is David Ray's analogy of "homemakers" and "housekeepers." A "homemaker" works on family relationships, security, and the maintenance of a warm and open environment. The "housekeeper" works with a job description to clean, arrange, and manage the house operation.

> Larger churches need and look for administrative or managerial qualities in potential leadership. The tasks are to build, coordinate, lead, and keep house. Smaller churches are in need of homemakers who can nurture, encourage, and enable the family members ... in larger program-conscious churches, the task or job to be done tends to take precedence.[16]

Another more popular ministerial model is Lyle Schaller's distinction between the "shepherd's" skills in a small church and a "rancher's" skills in a large church. The shepherd's skills are primarily relational, as he gives personal attention to the individual and is perceived to be a pastoral "lover." The rancher's skills are primarily functional, as he gives professional attention to the organization and is perceived to be a programmatic "leader." According to C. Peter Wagner, good pastors don't make churches grow, or they only grow so far as 200–250 maximum, unless the pastor changes his leadership style from shepherd to rancher or the shepherd-pastor leaves and is replaced by a rancher-pastor.

This does not mean that pastors of large churches love their congregations less than pastors of small churches. I can think of many pastors who are very expressive in their love for people regardless of the church size. But they are limited in terms of personal involvement with people, even though one superchurch pastor in Texas visits scores of Christmas parties in his church each year just to drop in and say hello. Another superchurch pastor in Michigan calls scores of people on the phone each week to pastorally socialize with them for a few minutes.

Making the shift from shepherd to rancher will most often require a change in the perspective of the people. In my first church after seminary, we grew from about 150 to 275 in seven years and started another church as well. I was expected to be at every official committee meeting. Once I left a Sunday school picnic planning meeting to follow up some converts, and I was criticized for it. Even though we built a new church and I enjoyed working with the building committee, after five years I asked the trustees to carry on without me. They protested that as pastor I should be with them.

In my next church of over five-hundred members I knew our people needed personal attention, so our first staff member to be added was an assistant pastor with major responsibilities for visitation and evangelism. Lyle Schaller says one of the most devisive issues in many churches today is pastoral calling because "in general the laity tend to put pastoral calling on members in their homes in the top third of the priorities for how a minister allocates his time. Ministers tend to place routine 'friendly' calling in the middle or bottom of the priorities for the pastor's time."[17] Despite my staff selection to provide pastoral visitation, people often expressed disappointment or criticism because the senior pastor had not visited them.

Sometimes the shift will require a change in the perspective of the pastor. He might be someone who relates more to people than he does to programs. He loves to be with his people, visit them when they're sick, chat with them after church, and have dinner in their homes. He loves pastoral work, but as his church grows, the more frustrated he becomes. His ministerial functions are too broad or are crowded out by his managerial functions. In some cases the pastor may not be able to change, but in other cases where he changes, he will also have to change the structure of his ministry.

THE STRUCTURAL MANAGEMENT OF GROWING CHURCHES

One succcessful example of this, the lay shepherding ministry, was developed by Baptist pastor Chuck Ver Straton. When his church in Colorado grew beyond his personal ability to pastor people, he said, "I was frustrated . . . ready to resign. My greatest strength had proved my undoing. God had given me a pastor's heart to care for people."[18] With more people to care for, he worked harder and then added more staff, but this only attracted more people. Finally, he initiated a lay-shepherding program which moved the management function of the deacons to another board, and he developed "people-type" deacons on their board in a three-year training program. Then finally he accepted the new role of leading shepherds rather than shepherding sheep. After he left the church, it continued to thrive under their pastoral care. If the church had been reluctant to reorganize it, it would have restricted growth potential even if their pastor was willing to change.

For example, Brethren Assemblies in New Zealand

that practice plural eldership have often plateaued at 150. Because of their inability to manage the ministry beyond that church growth ceiling, they have often split off into new churches. By contrast, Gary Inrig, a Brethren leader in Canada, has seen his church grow form 150 to 1,300 because they made the necessary structural changes. He admits that

> structures are significant. I wrestle with that because I emphasize very strongly the organic nature of the church life . . . but as our church has grown, I've realized that growth outruns administrative patterns and expresses administrative weaknesses. Many significant problems in Assemblies have arisen because we don't administer well.[19]

According to good management consultants, growing organizations should conduct an *annual* review of their structure to eliminate growth restrictions. It seems to me that churches that want to grow should do the same from time to time and should deal with two dimensions of structural management.

The Problems of Reorganization. In my experience, five problems might preclude positive restructuring.

1. Social Solidarity: Will change mean the loss of the intimacy inherent in the life of small and middle-sized churches?
2. Territorial Domain: Whose place in the structural space will be challenged by change?
3. Constitutional Cement: Will the changes be substantial or simple? (Unfortunately, too many constitutional documents are set in such detailed concrete they allow no functional flexibility for a growing organization.)

SCHALLER'S TYPOLOGY ON SIZE AND STRUCTURAL CHARACTERISTICS

Organizational Characteristics	Small Church (1–100)/10 Million Attend (33%)	Middle-Sized Church (100–200)/9 Million Attend (30%)	Large Church (200 +)/11 Million Attend (37%)
1. Government	Participatory democracy	Should become a representative democracy	Becomes a representative democracy
2. Decision Making	Power center in key families (family or clan)	Power center in key individuals (tribe: multiple families)	Power center in key positions and/or staff (nation)
3. Court of Appeal	Congregational meeting	Congregation and/or the governing board	Governing board
4. Change	Leading families or members	From minister through members, or from them	From pastoral staff or through them
5. Leadership	Responds	Interacts	Leads
6. Pastoral Role	Enabler	Team player	Leader coach
7. Pastoral-power	Little influence	Some influence	More influence
8. Lay Leadership	Some opinion maker and general overseer of the congregation	Too small for lay leaders to concede that the minister is in charge but too large to be lay controlled	In very large churches the minister assumes the role of the leader most in charge
9. Self-Image	Primary group: one big happy family	Like small church: big family but poor self-image	Corporation: many group structures
10. Focus of attention	People	Problems	Potential

Based on Lyle Schaller, *The Awkward Sized Church* (Nashville: Abingdon, 1984).

4. Maintenance Mentalities: Are people "looking in the rearview mirror" or looking ahead to change for the future?

5. Pastoral Paranoia: Are the people afraid of "pastor

power" or the loss of "people power" in the decision-making process of the church?

Evidence has been given that a strong leadership role by the pastor (and a board of elders) is often conducive to church growth, particularly as a church grows larger. Churches need to consider changing their management style to allow leaders more latitude to lead. Turning once again to Lyle Schaller's organizational analysis of churches for over twenty-five years, his typology on size and structural characteristics (see diagram) is extremely helpful in understanding this critical point.

The Principles of Reorganization. In the organizational development of church structures, I believe there are at least six concepts that can be conducive to growth.

A Single Board Structure: Based on the biblical concept of eldership, many churches today have enhanced their growth pattern through a single board system. A multiple board system with independent authorities faces potential problems with mutually exclusive ministry philosophies, lack of coordination, and lateral power conflicts (particulary over financial controls), and sometimes inconsistent spiritual standards for leadership. With appropriate authority to totally administer the ministry, this model is appropriate for any size church.

Management and Ministry Assignments: As churches grow, there often arises a practical conflict over these demands, if not a theological tension. When Chuck Ver Straton developed his lay-shepherding program, he found it necessary to assign administration to another board so his deacons could concentrate on pastoral care. When Gordon MacDonald's church boards had conflict over these functions, they reorganized with a board of directors to manage the church and a board of elders responsible for pastoral care and visitation, with no administrative functions. They split the functions because they "had learned from experience that when a person or board is charged with both, administration almost always overwhelms pastoral work."[20]

Eldership Rule and Deacon Ministries: When Charles H. Spurgeon reorganized his nineteenth-century Baptist church, he advocated that elders should rule and deacons should serve. In John MacArthur's church, the deacons carry out the directives of the elder board. The possible patterns here are multiple, but an important distinction needs to be maintained between general management (elders) and functional management (deacons).

Centralized and Decentralized Decision Making: It is axiomatic in management that policy making should be done at the top of an organizational unit, while policy implementation is done at a lower level. There needs to be balance here. Decentralization can endanger a unified ministry plan. On the other hand, centralization can develop a "decision drift" and "delegation drag" whereby management absorbs too much detail and too many decisions. I once consulted with a church that had grown from 30 to 1,000 in seven years and found their elder board was overinvolved in administrative details that could have been delegated out to other sub-committees.

Constitutional and Administrative Policies: Too many churches develop detailed structures in their constitutions that are not flexible enough for needed change. Legal considerations, denominational standards, and assignment of the administrative responsibilities for oversight of the ministry are essential but other demands might better be legislated by the board, simple bylaws, or policy handbooks that can be changed by those in charge as needed!

Standing Committees and Special Assignment: While I am not opposed to some standing committees, some of them just stand around while others work. With a flexible constitution, a board can do an annual audit on all committee and ministry functions. Another profitable pattern is the temporary appointment of task forces or selected leaders who can "ad hoc" others in their work. In addition, management decision-making committees should not overwhelm ministry action committees.

The Premise of Reorganization. The basic questions in church organizations are, Who does management? and Who does ministry? For a church to grow, it must allow more management authority to the pastor, the board, and the staff, and at the same time advocate more ministry for the people. The best book on this subject, *Leading Your Church to Growth*, advocates more management for the minister and more ministry for the people for a church to grow. The author, C. Peter Wagner, says elsewhere that the involvement of the congregation "needs to be concentrated on ministry functions rather than leadership functions. This is a very crucial point, for very little current writing in church leadership makes sufficient distinction between leadership roles and ministry roles."[21]

In conclusion, when a church reaches a growth ceiling and stagnant size, the minister-manager should analyze what problems exist in the following dimensions of his ministry to see what management solutions may be needed for church growth.

- *Spiritual:* Are people motivated and committed to church growth?
- *Social:* Are people's relational needs being met in the church?
- *Skills:* Do I need to change the way I manage the church?
- *Structure:* Does the church need to change the way it is managed for growth?

- *Staff:* Have we developed sufficient leadership for the church to grow?
- *Situation:* Is our ministry style appropriate to our market for growth?

In the next two chapters we shall discuss these last two dimensions of my church growth typology.

NOTES

1. Ted W. Engstrom, "What Good Managers Know," *Christian Leadership Letter,* February 1979, 1.
2. Lyle Schaller, *The Multiple Staff and the Larger Church* (Nashville: Abingdon, 1980).
3. Dan Martin, "Small New Churches More Effective," *Home Missions,* October 1978, 15.
4. Foster H. Shannon, *The Growth Crisis in the American Church: A Presbyterian Case Study* (Pasadena, Calif.: William Carey Library, 1977).
5. David A. Womack, *The Pyramid Principle* (Minneapolis: Bethany Fellowship, 1977), 69f.
6. Elmer Towns, *America's Fastest Growing Churches* (Nashville: Impact, 1972), 143.
7. Womack, *The Pyramid Principle,* 80.
8. Lyle E. Schaller, *Looking into the Mirror: Self Appraisal in the Local Church* (Nashville: Abingdon, 1984), 27.
9. Charles Mylander, *Secrets for Growing Churches* (San Francisco: Harper & Row, 1979), 115.
10. Win Arn, *The Win Arn Growth Report,* No. 14 (1986), 4.
11. Carl S. Dudley, *Making the Small Church Effective* (Nashville: Abingdon, 1978), 30.
12. Paul Beasley-Murray and Alan Wilkenson, *Turning the Tide* (London: British Bible Society, 1981), 45.
13. Moustafa H. Abdelsomed and Alexander T. Kindling, "Why Small Businesses Fail," *SAM Advanced Management Journal* (Society for Advancement of Management), Spring 1978, 26.
14. Ibid., 28.
15. Eddie Gibbs, *I Believe in Church Growth* (Grand Rapids: Eerdmans, 1981), 383.
16. David R. Ray, *Small Churches Are the Right Size* (New York: Pilgrim, 1982), 150.
17. Lyle E. Schaller, *The Decision Makers* (Nashville: Abingdon, 1974), 47.
18. Charles A. Ver Straton, *How to Start Lay-Shepherding Ministries* (Grand Rapids: Baker, 1983), 11.
19. Gary Inrig, "Between Trapezes: Growth Restrictors," *Insight* (Church of the Brethren), January 1987, 7.
20. Gordon MacDonald, "When Wineskins Start to Rip," *Leadership,* Winter 1984, 79.
21. C. Peter Wagner, "Good Pastors Don't Make Churches Grow," *Leadership,* Winter 1981, 71.

EIGHT

MORE THAN A
ONE-MAN SHOW:

STAFF AND MANAGEMENT

Organizations, be they nations, corporations, or churches, rise with the development of effective leadership. In *The Pyramid Principle*, David Womack graphically develops this universal management maxim for the church. Using the paradigm of a pyramid, he maintains a church cannot increase the "mass" of people it ministers to without first expanding its "base" of leadership in ministry and management. To try to do so is analogous to pouring sand on the center of a small square table until it eventually falls off the edges to the floor. Womack says,

> A minister with his staff and lay leaders can care for only a given number of people efficiently. When that efficiency level is reached, the church will cease to grow. . . . A church may try to grow past its administrative limitations, but it will always drop back to the level of efficiency of the pastor, staff and lay leaders.[1]

For Womack, this pyramid principle is the most important single factor in producing church growth.

The expression of this principle can be seen in three dimensions of church leadership, the first of which I would call *volunteer staff*. These are the unpaid lay leaders and workers of our church who give their time, talent, and treasure to the work. In the past few decades evangelicals have experienced a refreshing revival of interest in the Ephesians 4:12 pattern of "equipping of the saints for the work of service." Numerous articles and books have been written on the liberation of the laity. I have seen church letterheads that state, "Every member a minister." I have heard of a church where people do not become members unless they first sign up to be involved in some aspect of the ministry. Peter Wagner has also concluded that a "well mobilized laity" is the second vital sign of a healthy growing church, the first being a strong church growth pastor. Examples of this pattern in practice can be found in the United States and Canada as well as on the mission fields of the world.

An exciting example of this in the United States is the minstry of John Maxwell, senior pastor of the Skyline Wesleyan Methodist Church in San Diego, California. Speaking at a National Association of Evangelicals luncheon in 1985, he said the growth of his church was in direct proportion to the ministry ratio of his laity. In his church of 2,200, each Sunday the number of workers in 1985 was 780, an increase from 112 in 1981 when he assumed the pastorate there. Three important points were made about his model of lay mobilization: (1) From the moment a person becomes a member he should also be inducted into some form of ministry; (2) people, particularly leaders, should be discipled into effective evangelism in a life-related context; and (3) following the established principles of convincing communication, people are more motivated by what they see than what they hear.

When John Maxwell first began his ministry, he

preached three months on the pattern of Ephesians 4:12, thus establishing the biblical basis for the people to be equipped for the work of the ministry. (Being in a high crime area, even the parking attendent now knows he is doing what he does for Jesus and his church.) Maxwell's next step was to disciple his board members to become living models before the congregation. In his total pastoral ministry in three churches, up to that time forty-seven laymen had felt called of God into full-time Christian service. Ten of his eighteen board members at the time were making plans to arrange for their businesses to continue as they entered full-time Christian service.

Another exciting example is the Pentecostal church growth that has occurred in Colombia, South America. Here again, in many churches lay involvement and the use of spiritual gifts were prominent. Donald Palmer conducted a survey of fourteen different denominational leaders and twenty-six pastors and found the number one factor mentioned in church growth was the enthusiasm and activity of members who are motivated to develop their gifts, witness, and serve in the work.[2] In studying church growth in Latin America, one thing should be mentioned about mobilization. While not rejecting education in the schoolroom, they do emphasize experience in the streets. These "seminarios in the streets," as they are called, involve lay people in the practical ministries of old-fashioned street meetings, singing, giving testimonies, and speaking. This type of on-the-job training needs to be developed more in our American churches too. Volunteer staff development is essential for church growth.

Some missiologists suggest that volunteer staff on the mission field are in fact more important than vocational staff. Neil Braun, a Christian Advent missionary in Japan, stated that a major hindrance to church extension is requiring that each church *must* have a paid, trained pastor to function. He also states that the greater the number of paid staff, the lower the percentage of conversion growth. It is his conviction that on the mission field "the essential ministry is nonprofessional and the professional ministry is the supplemental one."[3]

This introduces a second dimension of leadership that needs to be developed both at home and abroad: *bivocational staff.* Following in the biblical tradition of "tentmakers" Aquila and Priscilla (Acts 18:2-3) and Paul (1 Cor. 9), these are the dedicated unpaid or low-paid pastors and workers who support themselves with other jobs to do the work of the ministry. I have seen pastors with the American Mission for Opening Closed Churches cramp their families into tiny trailers in the north woods of Maine, where they worked side by side with community lumberjacks, peeling bark off the trees to help earn a living. I have talked with black pastors in Chicago who sacrificially serve the Lord in their free time while working full-time to support themselves and their families.

There are also hosts of ethnic churches which would never have started or survived without the commitment of part-time clergy. The growth of the Southern Baptist Convention is due in part to almost ten thousand faithful bivocational pastors in ethnic, inner-city, rural, and mission churches in America. The growth of ethnic churches and "people group" churches around the world will be especially enhanced by these bivocational staff, both imported and indigenous.

The third dimension of leadership that needs to be developed is *vocational staff*: those paid staff in American churches commonly referred to as "multiple staff." The importance of this topic in my typology is found in the fact that while only 12 percent of Protestant churches have multiple staff (more than one full-time staff person), 50 percent of American church attenders go to these churches. If the average size American church is seventy-five members, then twenty average-size neighborhood churches in Chicago could attend Moody Church and only double a Sunday morning service of fifteen hundred to three thousand. Or, over fifty average size rural churches in northern Michigan could attend Ward Memorial Presbyterian Church outside Detroit and only double a series of Sunday morning services from four thousand to eight thousand. And all those people from Michigan could attend the Willow Creek Community Church in Barrington, Illinois, and only double its series of Sunday morning services from eight thousand to sixteen thousand or more. If churches are going to grow, then one major consideration is the subject of multiple staff.

THE NEED FOR MULTIPLE STAFF

There is a demand for more staff, particularly in evangelical churches. The commitment to evangelism in general, and church extension in particular, requires more clergy per capita. With the strong recruitment of workers for growing parachurch organizations, and the recycling of some of them into pastoral ministries, evangelical seminaries and schools have maintained increased enrollment while liberal seminary enrollment is on the decline. Warren Benson, vice-president of Trinity Evangelical Divinity School in Deerfield, Illinois, told me recently that there is an increase in the multiple staffs of evangelical churches, and the demand for more staff is far greater than the current supply of TEDS students, even though their number is also increasing. By contrast, Jackson Carroll, in his book *Too Many Pastors*, says there is a shrinking job market in liberal churches, where the pastoral supply is greater than the pulpit demand. He says in the National Council of Churches' mainline denominations the increasing cost of facilities, program, and staff is now raising some new questions about the validity of the full-time pastor as the standard role model.

Another impression I have is that the value of additional staff may be demonstrated in growing churches. Bill Yaeger of First Baptist Church, Modesto, California, has built a strong church on the philosophy that in order of priority it is first staff, then program, and last facilities. In 1977 I read a *Home Missions* magazine article about the top 425 fastest growing churches in the Southern Baptist Convention and noticed that two-thirds of those churches had one to three or more staff in addition to the pastor. I have also heard some experts say that capable staff members will result in more families that tithe, and that in one to two years the increased income will underwrite their salary.

One interesting study I have come across that seems to demonstrate this point is the study of British Baptist churches in the book *Turning the Tide*. Of 325 churches studied, 225 were one-man ministries and 46 were multiple-staff ministries, including support staff. The report concluded that where any type of multiple ministry is present there is a very definite bias toward growth. This report also said they found "a very strong link between churches that were growing and the availability of secretarial assistance to the ministry [and] a strong correlation between the employment of a full-time youth worker and the probability of the church being a growing one."[4]

THE NUMBER OF MULTIPLE STAFF

Various guidelines have been given about the number of staff a church should have in relationship to active membership, average Sunday morning worship attendance, and average Sunday school attendance. Over the past few decades the trend has been to reduce the ratio of staff to these standards of measurement. The result has been to require more multiple staff in churches for growth. In his book, *Multiple Church Staff Handbook*, Harold Westing makes the observation that "back in the Sixties, the magic number was 250–300 members per staff person. . . . In the Seventies the number dropped to 175–200. In the Eighties churches are adding staff when there are 125–150 new members."[5]

The current consensus is that there should be one staff member per 150–200 people being ministered to. People figures should also include those who do not always show up in the standard statistics. (The recent youth minister at Moody Church sometimes had as many as one hundred teenagers showing up for youth social programs, though less than half of them were in the Sunday school or worship services on any regular basis.)

THE NATURE OF MULTIPLE STAFF

While the addition of staff will not always cause a church to grow, the strategic addition of qualified staff should contribute to its growth. In his book *Managing for Results*, Peter Drucker says staffing decisions are the crucial decisions. "First-class people must always be allocated to major opportunites, to the areas of greatest possible return for each unit. And first-class opportunities must always be staffed with people of superior ability and performance."[6] The selection of the right person for a staff position is part of Drucker's "crucial decision," but the strategy for the right position to staff is also important. We are told by church growth consultants that most churches are understaffed for growth. As such, there are at least four areas of staff development that should be considered for church growth.

Secretarial Staff Development. When I was about to leave my first church after seminary to go to my next

e, a multiple-staff situation, an experienced
_iend said my first consideration should be a
good full-time secretary. There was wisdom in these
words, and many pastors in churches with 100 to 200
members in particular would be helped by a full- or
part-time secretary. I certainly appreciated the two
spare-time secretaries in my first church, which grew to
275, as well as the full-time secretaries in my next
church. Charles Mylander reports on a study done
years ago on 9,000 churches by Richard Myers which
demonstrated the need for a full-time secretary for each
minister and 200 people.[7] Certainly, this can be one of
the keys to breaking through the so-called 200 barrier.

Specialized Staff Development. Some Christian education leaders have observed that many evangelical
churches will first add program staff in the areas of
Christian education and youth work. Some suggest it is
probably best to hire a Christian education director
first, but often churches will hire youth directors first. In
some circles, a position is often created for a Christian
education/music director. Win Arn, himself a former denominational Christian education executive, says, however, that if

> a youth worker, Christian education director or mu-
> sic director, etc., is added as the first professional
> person after the pastor, their work is usually inter-
> nal. Additional people are not reached in sufficient
> numbers for the budget to grow to keep the
> church and staff growing, and a plateaued church
> is often the result.[8]

Arn, who now gives direction to the Institute for
American Church Growth, says the first staff position
for growth should be a person in evangelism.

Sequential Staff Development. When the question arises as to whether or not there is a uniform pattern of staff development, there are differing opinions. For example, in his book *Twelve Keys to an Effective Church*, Callahan suggests the following order for staff development: (1) the pastor, (2) director of music, (3) church secretary or church administrator, (4) program directors, and then, last, (5) director of mission and outreach. He recognizes that churches vary but says, "The order mentioned above is a useful sequence for a majority of congregations which are seeking to grow or are already growing."[9] On the other hand, Marvin Rickard, whose church in southern California grew from 83 to 6,500, says, "We have never developed a chart or priority list of the ideal order of staff growth."[10] While patterns of staff development may be useful, principles are probably more important, particularly as they relate to the philosophy of ministry that is being pursued for church growth.

Strategic Staff Development. The crucial choice of staff positions may be best determined by answering at least three basic questions. First of all, What is the style and strength characteristics of the pastor? If a church is prepared to build its ministry on strengths, which it should do, the starting point is the pastor. Although there are some legitimate role expectations for every pastor, each one is uniquely created by God with a combination of gifts, personality, and a personally developed philosophy of ministry. Before taking a position of negative criticism, where possible a church should be positive and seek to complement the pastor's style and weak points in its development of staff positions.

The second question is, What are the needs of the situation at that time in the life of the church? Needs assessment, however, should focus both on the church *and* the community. I consulted with a church in the Wheaton area where the third full-time position was filled by an effective youth pastor who was not only ministering to church kids but reaching out to scores more in the community. The families of children and youth being reached in that total ministry have since become a "primary prospect list" for adult evangelism.

3RD

The third question is, What is the strategy and philosophy of ministry being developed for church growth? Here there should be two main concerns which in fact can complement each other: equipping ministries and evangelistic ministries. In 1976 a British minister did a study of four American churches with significant growth patterns: (1) the Church of the Savior in Wayne, Pennsylvania, a new church which grew from zero to seven hundred in four years, (2) Peninsula Bible Church, which had grown to three thousand under Ray Stedman's ministry, (3) the First Baptist Church of Modesto, California, which had grown to two thousand in eight years under Bill Yaeger's ministry, and (4) the Fellowship Bible Church in Dallas, Texas, a new church which had grown from zero to three thousand in four years under Gene Getz's ministry. His observation was that one key factor in all their growth patterns was strategic staff development. He said, "They were concerned with multiple leadership and put their money into this. Around fully qualified and highly trained lay leaders the full-time staff spent much of their time building themselves into lay leaders. The lay leaders were in each church called elders."[11]

Donald McGavran, father of the church growth movement, says there are two primary classes of church lay leadership. Class I leaders direct their energies primarily toward the maintenance of the organized ministry in the church. Class II leaders direct their energies primarily toward the mission of an outreach ministry in the community. To enhance church growth, sufficient numbers of Class II leaders need to be developed. Class II workers must be somewhere between 10 and 20 percent of the active membership for the church to be really growing in most cases. In a study of six fast-growing churches in part of one western state, in at least four of the churches the pastoral staff provided training for Class II leaders. In all the churches, the percentage of people who were active in bringing people to Christ was at least 12 percent, and in two churches was as much as 25 percent.

In both of the above cases, pastoral staff were committed to the development of people in ministry and mission. This raises an important question about strategies and methods beyond the purpose of this chapter, but there is one important point that needs to be made here. Developing Class II leaders requires developing pastoral staff who are themselves committed to a personal evangelistic life-style, particularly as they seek to be models to the people, not just managers of persons for evangelism.

I shall never forget the admonition of Stephen Olford, who once exhorted the pastors at a conference never to hide behind the pulpit when it comes to personal evangelism. While it is true that not every pastor has the gift of evangelism (Eph. 4:11), a pastor should "do the work of an evangelist," as seen in Paul's exhortation to Timothy (2 Tim. 4:5). Recently the training director of CBMC shared a Life-style Evangelism Seminar with the leaders of an evangelical denomination and found most of them had few unsaved friends that they were trying to reach for Christ. If a pastor and his staff say they wish to reach a neighborhood or city for Christ, it ought to be a number one priority in their lives to be in personal contact with people *outside* the church who need Christ. This theme will be further developed later in the book, but the fourth area of staff development should now be discussed.

THE NURTURE OF MULTIPLE STAFF

In attempting to provide some guidelines for pastors, I would like to briefly identify some critical issues in the management of multiple staff. These issues deal with the staff person in relationship to their position, the organization structure, their style, and their supervision.[12]

Staff Selection. As we have noted in the words of Peter Drucker, staffing decisions in an organization are crucial decisions. This naturally raises two key questions. Where may new staff be located? and Who should the new staff person be? At Moody Church some staff positions were filled by people inside the congregation: a retired bookkeeper who served as a full-time volunteer on the office staff, a seminary graduate who became a part-time intern in discipleship, and an enthusiastic contractor who was hired as the camp director. At other times, outside sources can be utilized, such as school alumni and placement services, district or denominational offices, InterCristo, classified ads in Christian magazines, personal referrals, or a host of other contacts.

In order to decide who the new staff person should be, I would suggest a seven-point plan that I have found helpful in recruiting and recommending staff.

Prayer. Since God chooses which gifts (1 Cor. 12) and calling (Acts 13, 16) to give men, and gives those men to His church (Eph. 4), it is essential that we pray for His will in the selection of staff. I was once asked by a friend what the prospects were to be chosen for a position I was interested in. I replied that if it were God's will, it was 100 percent positive, but if it wasn't His will, the possibilities were zero. One outstanding example of answered prayer in this regard for me occurred in my first pastorate in 1969, when the Lord led my wife and me to develop an additional coffeehouse ministry during the hippie revolution. In time, I desperately needed an associate with whom to share the ministry. With no financial assistance available from the church, God nevertheless supplied the need. He sent me an experienced pastor who was ready to resign a successful pastorate and come to work alongside me as the bivocational director of "His House" Ministries. Although he never received any salary from the church, in due time, through gifts and other sources, he became full-time director of the ministry. Now, one of my closest friends, he is the pastor of an International Church in San Juan, Puerto Rico, where he continues to bring people to the Lord Jesus Christ.

Patience. More than one manager or minister has made the mistake of hasty staff selection. As I recruited and recommended staff at Moody Church, I found the process could take from six months to a year. Even though, in the meantime, I became acting business manager, singles administrator, and radio ministry administrator, I found good staff were worth waiting for.

Position. A good job description defining both responsibility and authority is essential. Review it carefully with the candidate! I have heard of pastors or staff members who became frustrated and disillusioned because what happened in practice did not match what was on paper. The fine print, as well as the "hidden agenda," are both critical to the contract.

Portfolio. In addition to written resumes and references, take time to use the telephone or meet in person to talk to people about a candidate. Not all promising candidates look so well after research. Professional personnel directors often assume that the best predictor of future behavior is past performance. Of course, the personal interview is essential, but other opportunities to observe a person "in action" should be considered. In an article on "How to Pick a New Executive," the author says, "The difficult part of an executive search is measuring the attributes that cannot be learned from a resume."[13] He provides weekend vacations with candidates for further first-hand observation.

Personality. Personality tests are back. Although these are often used in executive development, I am now committed to their use in staff selection as well. Some Christian organizations use the popular Myer-Briggs test, and Intercristo recommends PMI's Motivated Abilities Pattern, but I use the Biblical Personal Profile System from Performax, mentioned in chapter 5. The significance of these tools will be seen later.

Philosophy of Ministry. It is important not only to match the gift-mix of a candidate with a position but to match the philosophy of ministry as well. In particular, there should be a thorough discussion of the pastor's philosophy of ministry, the staff modus operandi, and the church administrative structure for staff and board/committee relationships especially.

Perception. In some respects, there is a skill in staff selection. Sufficient and effective questions must be asked. Strengths and weaknesses must be discerned. An accounting executive that I led to the Lord a few years ago says that in his staff selection he does not assume basic character can be changed on the job, but given the right attitude and basic aptitude, the competency level can be increased. We should build on the person's strengths so long as the weaknesses are not too prominent or pertinent to acceptable performance standards. As in the beginning, through the process, and especially at the point of a crucial staffing decision, prayer should be a priority in selecting the right person for a particular staff position. The next critical issue in multiple staff management is: How does the staff person fit into the organizational structure?

Staff Structures. This refers to the relationship a staff person has to the senior pastor and the church board and to committee leadership structure. As I have already noted, leadership styles vary. But for the sake of illustration, I would identify at both ends of the spectrum two staff operational styles. The first would be a command staff structure. As one example, Jack Hyles believes the staff is an enlargement of the pastor, and he requires 100 percent unquestioned loyalty of them. He believes there should never be any doubt expressed by a staff member concerning the pastor and his work. According to his *Church Manual*, staff members should each have an assigned area of responsibility and be given confidence to do it. Since in his case the pastor is the overseer of the entire church program, "no staff member should pursue a program without the pastor's approval. He should oversee and approve anything that goes on."[14]

At the other end of the spectrum is the "collegial" staff structure. Ken Mitchell once described this as the condition whereby staff members would negotiate openly their relative roles. (It reminds one of the cartoon in *Leadership* magazine where three pastors are casting lots to see who goes with the junior high kids to camp.) One Baptist pastor who supports this style says, "The entertainment world has room for a star supported by a cast of backups, but I do not believe this is the biblical model. I do not want to see my colleagues as 'my staff' who assist me as I carry on 'my ministry' in 'my church.'"[15] While many collegial models maintain that the ministry is still under the coordination of the senior pastor, some attempts have been made to maintain co-pastor collegial models. Though some attempts have been made to pursue a pure pattern like this, the true team efforts have been few and far between, and often something comes between the members of the team. (Interestingly enough, in 1878, a Constitutional Amendment was proposed that the office of President should be replaced with an executive council of three men, but obviously it was overturned.)

Still, a trend has been taking place in executive management that should at least be noted. In a recent article entitled "Who's in Charge?" the author describes the new "smart team" management.

> The term ."smart team" is loosely defined as a group of senior executives who work well together and who have distinct and complementary talents. Regardless of the title, members of a team share the responsibility of CEO. No one member of the team has veto power—all decisions are reached by consensus. Three heads are better than one. A smart team will make more effective decisions because its members are forced to think through differences, gather more accurate data, and reach an agreement. . . . In the 1960s and 1970s, many major corporations began experimenting with the group management concept, creating teams with such labels as "Office of the Chief Executive," "Corporate Management Committee," and "Corporate Office." As of 1980, more than one-third of the Fortune 500 companies had some form of an office of the chief executive.[16]

Of course, there are quite a range of options along the spectrum with the command staff model at one end and the collegial staff model at the other end. And there can be problems with each one. I heard of one large church with a command model where the senior pastor single-handedly fired a new, yet experienced, staff member simply because he didn't "fit." There was no pastoral relations committee to stand by the man. On the other hand, if no one is really in charge of the staff you have the problem of a real leadership vacuum. Even Robert Worley, who strongly advocates collegial ministry in churches, admits that there are few church organizations which have developed this model. He says even the senior minister may have remarkable sensitivities about human relations, but the organizational expectations of him as a leader with particular dominant, charismatic, chief executive, or line officer style influences his behavior in relation to his peers.[17]

My point in describing these models is not to advocate one extreme or the other. My concern is this: Staff members must not only be able to fit into a particular position, they must also feel compatible with the organizational structures. Of course, this also includes their relationships to boards and committees. I personally find some organizational structures in churches unacceptable. A cardinal rule in most management circles is that no executive or employee occupying a single position in the organization should be subject to orders from more than one source. And yet examples abound in churches where staff people are responsible to the senior pastor and someone else.

In one church where I was senior pastor, the minister of music and youth was responsible to the music committee under the deacon board, the Christian education board for youth, and myself. In another church, the camp director was responsible to the associate pastor, the camp committee, the trustee board who assumed overall responsibilities for the physical facilities and grounds, the finance committee for financial policies, and the business manager who ran the office support staff, not to mention a working relationship with the Christian education administrator as well. I prefer the model of John MacArthur's church, where a pastoral elder is responsible for each ministry unit and is assisted by a lay elder, or the model of another large church in the Midwest where all ministry is under the direction of staff whose general oversight is developed by the senior pastor and elder board. When I hear of churches where the staff member is responsible to a lay elder for his ministry even though there is a senior pastor, I feel the cardinal rule has again been broken. But my main point is that effective staff development must have staff who fit both the position in ministry as well as the philosophy of ministry organizationally. The next crucial issue after selection and structure is style.

Staff Styles. The subject of style is another crucial issue in staff development for two major reasons, the first of which is the position a staff member holds. What are the role expectations that go along with the job description? For example, in an examination of effective youth workers, more of them are rated "people-oriented" than "task-oriented." Their motto might be "I am ministering to people not managing a program!" As such, some successful youth workers might well be expected not to be such effective administrators. Unfortunately, they may even be criticized by their kids for being disorganized. So you need to build on that youth worker's strengths but also provide a strong, close supervision system and able administrative support staff.

The second reason why style is so important is because of the other people on the staff team and how they will relate to each other. While I was acting business manager at Moody Church for almost a year, I found that the office staff organization was never static. With changes in staff came subsequent changes in responsibilities and the dynamics of interpersonal relationships. Even in a modest command structure, the communication process and unidentified power plays can change. One solution to the problem is to recognize and respond to the distinctives of spiritual gifts. In describing his "Model for Multiple Staff Management," Kent Hunter said, "Spiritual gifts became the modus operandi in our executive staff."[18] As I have said, I find the Biblical Personal Profile most effective for me in understanding some of the dynamics and needs of multiple-staff management.

If minister-managers of multiple staff are to be effective church growth pastors, it is imperative they investigate the dynamics of multiple-staff relationships.[19] The reason I have briefly focused on staff selection, staff structures, and staff styles is because they are fundamental to my final point for a positive multiple-staff management experience. Good staff supervision is greatly enhanced by a mature comprehension of those issues.

Staff Supervision. Having been a senior pastor in two churches with some multiple staff, and an executive associate pastor in a large church with nine other staff, I know that task of staff supervision in a local church is a tremendous challenge to a pastor's leadership. Peter Wagner says that many pastors do not have the ability to lead a staff effectively. And commentary on the subject is not always positive. Some say, "Multiple-staff tensions are not uncommon." Others report that "staff disease" is a rather common ailment among pastors in major denominations where staff members move, on the average, every two years or less. A few years ago, the newly appointed secretary of a denominational church administration board said staff relations were probably the most elusive and difficult problem facing churches with large multiple staff.

Consider these statements: (1) One denominational secretary in southern California told me that three-quarters of multiple-staff relationships with senior pastors he knew were not considered positive because senior pastors were threatened by a strong staff. (2) A study of ministers of education in one denomination found that a major cause of job stress was conflict with the pastor or pastoral staff. (3) In another study the most frequently mentioned job stress factors were conflicts with the congregation (76 percent) or with other staff (56 percent). In that particular report, associate pastors had the greatest number of combined problems which were "interrelated with a failure of their dreams to be realized and unrealistic expectations of their senior pastor. Over 60 percent experienced disappointment or depression in relation to the continuous pressure which they experienced."[20]

Multiple-staff ministries provide great potential for growth, but, as we have seen, they can produce problems as well. Before accepting a staff position, a candidate should seek a clear definition of his or her responsibilities and the relationships he or she will enter with the senior pastor, the other staff, and the structures they will be required to work through. On the other hand, when a minister-manager becomes a senior pastor of a church, he should not assume the modus operandi he used in his former church needs no adjustment to his new church. And if he has never been a senior pastor, he should make every effort to learn how to be an effective minister-manager of multiple staff if he wants his church to grow. I hope this chapter provided some guidelines for that purpose.

NOTES

1. David A. Womack, *The Pyramid Principle* (Minneapolis: Bethany Fellowship, 1977), 80-81.
2. Donald Palmer, "The Growth of the Pentecostal Churches in Colombia" (D. Miss. diss., Trinity Evangelical Divinity School, 1972), 114.
3. Neil Braun, *Laity Mobilized: Reflections on Church Growth in Japan and Other Lands* (Grand Rapids: Eerdmans, 1971).
4. Paul Beasley-Murray and Allan Wilkinson, *Turning the Tide* (London: British Bible Society, 1981), 38.

5. Harold J. Westing, *Multiple Church Staff Handbook* (Grand Rapids: Kregel, 1985), 149.
6. Peter F. Drucker, *Managing for Results* (New York: Harper & Row, 1964), 150.
7. Charles Mylander, *Secrets for Growing Churches* (San Francisco: Harper & Row, 1979), 58.
8. Win Arn, *Church Growth America* (American Institute for Church Growth, Pasadena, California), January-February 1979, 12.
9. Kennon L. Callahan, *Twelve Keys to an Effective Church* (San Francisco: Harper & Row, 1983), 46-49.
10. Marvin G. Rickard, *Let It Grow: Your Church Can Chart a New Course* (Portland Ore.: Multnomah, 1984), 112.
11. Michael Caddock, "Eldership," *Church Growth Digest* 6 (British Church Growth Association), Winter 1984-1985, 1-3.
12. Many good resources are available on the subject of multiple staff management. These include *The Multiple Staff and the Larger Church,* by Lyle Schaller (Nashville: Abingdon, 1980); and *Multiple Church Staff Handbook,* by Harold Westing (Grand Rapids: Kregel, 1985); and *Church Staff Administration: Practical Approaches,* by Leonard Wedel (Nashville: Broadman, 1978).
13. Russel S. Reynolds, "How to Pick a New Executive," *Fortune,* 1 September 1986, 113.
14. Jack Hyles, *The Hyles Church Manual* (Murfreesboro, Tenn.: Sword of the Lord, 1973), 273ff.
15. Harry Clemens, "The Pastoral Staff as a Ministry Team," *Review and Expositor,* Winter 1981, 52.
16. Abagail W. Reifsynder, "Who's in Charge?" *Success,* November 1986, 49.
17. Robert G. Worley, "Collegial Ministry in Parish Organizations" (Class material, McCormick Theological Seminary, n.d.).
18. Kent R. Hunter, "A Model for Multiple Staff Management," *Leadership,* Summer 1981, 104.
19. In addition to the resources mentioned in chapter 5, I would recommend *Pastor's Handbook on International Relationships,* by Jard DeVille (Grand Rapids: Baker, 1965) and *Ministers as Leaders,* by Robert Dale (Nashville: Broadman, 1984).
20. Craig W. Ellison and William S. Mattila, "The Needs of Evangelical Leaders in the United States," *Journal of Psychology and Theology* 11, Spring 1984, 30.

NINE

YOUR CHURCH AND THE LOCAL MARKETPLACE:

SITUATION AND MANAGEMENT

Situational analysis for ministry is fundamental to church growth. In previous chapters I have shared some pastoral examples showing the need for some management "style-flex" within the guidelines of biblical principles, sound organizational practice, and the personal profile of the pastor and the people he works with. The aim of this chapter is to go one step further into the field of marketing to show the importance of developing a "style-flex" for ministry as well.

CHURCH AND COMMUNITY CHARACTERISTICS

Many church growth consultants stress the need for a situational analysis of a church and its community setting. They assume that each church has a distinctive set of characteristics that makes it more or less effective in its community. In *Your Church Has Personality*, Kent Hunter defines this as a philosophy of ministry but says "the problem is that most congregations do not know they are unique. Worse, they do not know why. They don't understand what it is that makes them so

178

special. They have never consciously spelled out their philosophy of ministry."[1]

Certainly there are biblical mandates for any local church. Some have prioritized them as worship, discipleship, and evangelism, and others add social service. However, there is more to discerning a distinctive philosophy of ministry than simply setting priorities. For example, some churches with evangelism as a priority operate a "front door" ministry where evangelistic activities center in the church, while other churches operate a "side door" ministry where evangelism is centered outside the church. The following three methods might help the minister-manager as he tries to define the philosophy of ministry in his particular church.

People assessment procedures. Many denominations and church growth organizations have developed research tools like surveys, rating scales, and opinion polls to see what a congregational consensus might be. This often provides an insightful information data base for decision making. However, I believe ultimately a well-defined philosophy of ministry must be established and articulated by leadership.

Program analysis. This option provides a practical supplement to surveys if it asks the right questions about what really is, not what is perceived or preferred to be. What programs are in operation? Which ones are in practice most important and why? How much time, money, and staff are expended on these programs? What is preached and promoted in the pulpit? This "spiritual energy audit" may prove revealing.

Particular typology awareness. During this last decade many contributions have been made to classify churches into typologies. The reason this is so important is that growth strategies must be based on knowing what kind of church is ministering in what kind of community. In their excellent exploration of typologies, Daniel Reeves and Ron Jenson say,

Understanding the advantages and limitations of a particular strategy in a specific situation will continue to be one of the most critical aspects of developing a good plan for church growth. One of the chief reasons most churches don't grow is that they are using the wrong game plan.[2]

Another approach to understanding a local church philosophy of ministry may be found in the current concept of "corporate culture." The originators of this concept a few years ago say values are its basis. One author defines it as "the pattern of basic assumptions that the group has invented, discovered, or developed in learning to cope with its problems of external adaptation and internal integration."[3] These values in consumer terms might be customer satisfaction or quality first products, and cultures usually take time to build. One of the hottest new options on the job market today is that of a corporate culture identity consultant.

In his book *Managing Corporate Culture*, Stanley Davis says successful companies place a great emphasis on values and generally have three characteristics. (1) They have a clear, explicit philosophy about how they aim to conduct their business. (2) Management pays a great deal of attention to shaping and fine-tuning these values and communicating them to the organization. (3) These values are shared by those who belong to the organization. Davis also notes one other critical factor that is applicable to the minister-manager: "Guiding beliefs are invariably set at the top and transmitted down the ranks. Any effort to change them must be led by the chief executive."[4] Finally, it is often observed that declining organizations too often have basic assumptions that no longer apply in a changed situation.

An example of defining a total church "corporate culture" might be found in the case of many fast-growing

Baptist Bible Fellowship churches. As I have analyzed them, they have three distinctive characteristics or basic values that work together. (1) In their priority of evangelism they are *aggressive* in using methods of house-to-house visitation, Sunday school, and, in the past, bus ministries. (2) In their philosophy of the pastor, he is *autocratic,* often entrepreneurial in nature, evangelistic in the pulpit, and on top of an executive pyramidal organization. (3) In their position of separation from the world, they are usually *militant,* stressing high standards for workers and staff, the fundamentals of Bible doctrine, and the independence of the local church. As successful as they are, though, some of their methods will not work well in certain situations.

Assuming an analysis is conducted, critical "match-factors" must then be evaluated between the church and community relative to a philosophy of ministry and church growth potential. Since growth most often occurs along homogeneous lines, and preference is not always prejudice, the correlation for probable success is often quite simple and positive. When the suburban exodus from the cities took place a few decades ago, new communities became fertile fields for church extension. Denominations like the Presbyterians found in their research that they could predict growth for their churches in communities that were characterized by growth in single-family residences and school populations, economic expansion, and an affluent Anglo culture.

Conversely, research has also demonstrated that many churches will decline when their communities change. In a study of 100 Southern Baptist churches, declining churches no longer reflected their communities sociologically, economically, racially, nationally, ethnically, or in age patterns. Interestingly enough, the philosophy of ministry affected the rate of decline. Churches with a priority of evangelism declined about

47 percent, churches with a combination of evangelism and social ministry declined about 73 percent, while churches with a priority on social ministry declined 87 percent. The major problem was the lack of commitment on the part of church members to meet the challenge.[5] Since then many others have described these churches as "the ex-neighborhood church" (Schaller), "the changing church" (Arn and McGavran), the church dying of "ethnikitis" (Wagner), a "closed system" church (Jones), or a "sealed-off" church (Schuller).

One pioneer in the field of church and community analysis is Douglas Walrath. In 1977 he completed a twenty-five-year study to develop a social context typology for twelve types of communities. He demonstrated that each type had its own peculiar pattern of social change. By identifying each community, he could forecast with some certainty how variable "match-factors" like medium age, male professional leadership, income, or mobility would affect both the rate and type of change that in turn impacted church growth. He drew the simple conclusion that "a decline in congregations is related to the widening social distance between the church and its immediate neighborhood."[6]

Another important ingredient to mention is that of the pastor-people relationship. In most growing churches the pastor functionally fits the "sociological," "eth-class," or "homogeneous" characteristics of the congregation. Some research also suggests that leadership effectiveness is often contingent on a congruence between the role expectations of the pastor and the people, with attendance being a positive by-product of a good match. Walrath found that churches suffering most from adverse social change often lacked qualified pastoral leadership. Regarding a suitable style, churches going through the crisis of a changing situation particularly need strong pastors who will wisely and willingly lead their churches through or to change.

I have observed that it is not a time for laissez-faire leadership. Even persistent, but passive, pastoral leadership may fail to effect a "corporate turnaround," although in some cases the pastor serves the role of attending physician and possible funeral director for the church if it dies.

Peter Wagner has said that

> while Americans indoctrinated with the melting pot theory of social reality are typically reluctant to talk about differences or regional origin, class, race, education, economic status, ethnicity, and the like, these factors are nevertheless highly important in predicting whether a pastor-parish match will succeed. . . . Generally speaking, the growth potential will be higher when the new pastor has a sociological orientation similar to that of most members of the congregation.[7]

In some cases, the pastor must be a slight sociological cut above. But what happens when the pastor is like the people and they are both unlike the community?

A case study occurred a few years ago in Bell-Maywood, California, which might be called "The Tale of Two Churches." Historically, this urban community had been a white middle-class residential area but was going through a transition as many lower-class white workers and diverse Hispanic groups moved in. One church changed and grew while the other church did not change or grow. A question arises: If one of the churches wanted to reach the white lower-class workers, they needed a new pastor. But should the pastor be matched with the lower-class community or the middle-class church? The writer of this case study said a mismatch was unavoidable. If matched with the church, the minister would be mismatched with the community, and vice versa. If the church was to grow, it probably meant that either the pastor must be matched with the community for maximum growth potential, or he must be committed to the mission of making a transition for another pastor to follow. He concluded that "the matching of the pastor to the community is second only to the fact and extent of homogeneity as a prime factor in growth."[8]

MARKETS AND MARKETTES

Depending on the nature and rate of community change, some churches have been caught in the trauma of transition without adapting to, much less anticipating, the change. In the words of Tom Peters (*In Search of Excellence*), they failed to stay "close to the customer." They operated from a *reactive* position rather than a *proactive* perspective. In the words of Paul, they did not say, "To the Jews, I became as a Jew . . . I have become all things to all men that I may by all means save some (1 Cor. 9:19-22). In other words, they did not define the style of their ministry by the situation in their market. As such, I want to provide an extended elementary introduction to the sophisticated world of marketing to show how the minister-manager might use it as a useful tool to accomplish his task.

The Mind-set of Marketing. Whereas sales had typically focused on production and promotion, in the early fifties the marketing concept developed to focus more on the perceived needs of people. The classic remark of Henry Ford that people could have any color Ford they wanted so long as it was black eventually proved both unrealistic and unprofitable. Simply stated, a market is an identifiable group of people who share a common need. However homogeneous that might be though, they will utilize a variety of sources or services to satisfy that need. A "markette" is a much more narrowly defined segment of that group. For example, radio broadcasters provide "narrow-casting," or "market segmentation," so listeners can turn the dial to whatever style sound they prefer. Professional marketing managers try to define and determine "target markets," or smaller "markettes," for tailor-made services or products. Robert Schuller of the Crystal Cathedral has conducted his church for years on the philosophy of "Find a need and fill it." A few years ago, Ralph Neighbour, Jr., wrote *Target Group Evangelism* with this same mind-set to develop a small group ministries to people with "special" felt needs. Whether it be through a church or a small group, markets or markettes can be targeted for ministry.

The Data Base of Demographics. Whereas demographics originally developed as a framework for social analysis, it moved from the classroom to the boardroom when business saw its relevance to sales. Demographics defines population characteristics in categories of geography, age, gender, income, occupation, education, religion, race, and ethnicity. Social stratification is one of its most important broad variables. New ethnographic studies can also enrich our understanding of cultural subgroups for effective evangelism.

The Patterns of Psychographics. In 1963 a new three-dimensional model was introduced to understand people's activities, interests, and opinions. Later labeled as "Life-style Patterns," this model combined (a) demographics, (b) social class, and (c) psychological characteristics. Demography was integrated with psychology, and by 1975 there were at least thirty-two different life-style definitions. In 1978, Arnold Mitchell introduced the VALS systems (life-styles and values) which identified four major groups in America. One of those was a large group of "outer-directed" people who were belongers or achievers. A second fast-growing group was "inner-directed" people who were experiential or societally conscious. Recently, a marketing service called "Clusterplus" advertised information that was now available on forty-seven highly distinctive life-style clusters. Psychographic research is still attempting to upgrade the VALS system because the population has changed since then. These professional "environmental scanners" (situational analysts) want to develop even more sophisticated psychographic systems for future marketing.

As an example in marketing, the VALS system was effectively used recently by a developer to build and market homes in Texas. Homes that provided sensible luxury and technology attracted the "achiever" market. Homes with big kitchens and family-life advertising attracted the "belonger" market. Ads for homes showing a young couple eating an ethnic meal on the living room floor attracted the "societally conscious" customer. As an example in ministry, urbanologist Ray Bakke said that growing urban churches respond to three basic felt-needs. "Existential" churches who are charismatic or creative attract people who want to live in the "now" or "new" dimension of life. "Relational" churches who are small, or have small groups, attract people who want a few close friends or extended families. "Goal-oriented" churches attract middle-management professionals and achiever types.

One major market that should be targeted for ministry today is the baby boomer generation of 75 million people born between 1945 and 1964. From 1957 to the period of 1976-1986, the national fertility rate (births per thousand women) dropped 50 percent and created what is now being called "the birth dearth." The 1973 Supreme Court decision to legalize abortion, singles' search for success that postpones marriage or motherhood in favor of career, and two-career families have influenced this greatly. As a result, in 1985 the median age in America increased to over thirty, and the largest population group was between twenty and forty. A special segment (markette) of this market would be single-parent families, predominately made up of women. Between 1965 and 1985, their number doubled (10.1 to 22.2 percent) while births to unmarried women tripled (7.7 percent to 28.7 percent). One pastor told me almost half the adult families in his area were single-parent families, but his church seems disposed at this time to make their second staff person a youth pastor.

A survey of the values and views of the baby boomer generation shows a definite trend toward secularization that presents a real challenge to the church. Here's what some social analysts say:

- According to *Not Like Our Fathers*, it is estimated that 80 percent of baby boomers embrace "libertine views." Situation ethics has become the standard for the secular mind-set.
- According to *Psychology Today*, "Twenty years ago more than 80 percent of college freshmen said that developing a meaningful philosophy of life was an important or essential goal. Today only 41 percent of freshmen consider that goal worthy."[9] Now materialism is the major purpose, while at the same time depression is considered a major problem in this age group.
- According to Robert Bellah, there are now four major philosophies of life in our society, two of which David McKenna identifies as devoted to "radical self-interest": (1) utilitarian individualism, which pursues pleasure and profit, and (2) expressive individualism, which pursues personal potential.
- According to Daniel Yankelovich, this new breed of

adults was not likely to raise their children with the same set of traditional family values we have had in America in the previous generations.

Still, some churches are reaching out to this market with success. A few years ago *Leadership* magazine surveyed 700 church visitors who were called on by evangelism teams in three different churches. Of these, 62 percent were in the 20–35 age bracket and 80 percent of new believers came from this group. Author Marshall Shelley said, "Possibly this can be explained because the early adult years are transition years, and those in flux are more receptive to the gospel."[10] Recently the Woodale Church of Minneapolis, Minnesota, relocated their large church and restructured their style of ministry to reach this group. Speaking recently at an NAE workshop entitled "Reaching the Baby Boomer Generation," pastor Leith Anderson outlined some important assumptions they made in their analysis and adaptation of ministry. Based on some correspondence he had with Lyle Schaller on characteristics of churches that were effective with baby boomers, he noted that these churches

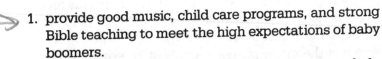

1. provide good music, child care programs, and strong Bible teaching to meet the high expectations of baby boomers.
2. build on the "reciprocity" of baby boomers to help them become responsible church members.
3. usually have a positive pattern of growth and are over five hundred in size.
4. provide a strong singles ministry.

Just as Woodale Church has been successful in target marketing the baby boomer generation, so other churches can be more successful in targeting markets in their ministry community by following the simple

DEFINING THE MINISTRY COMMUNITY	
1. DEFINE MINISTRY AREA	• Plot membership on map • Determine distances you can expect people to travel. • Fix a geographical area using this travel distance.
2. DESCRIBE POTENTIAL MINISTRY PEOPLES	• Identify the distinctive groups in the ministry area. • Describe each of these in detail.
3. UNDERSTAND YOUR CHURCH PROFILE	• Consider attitudes of members, age and education, interest of members, building facilities, philosophy of ministry, financial resources, gift-mix, leadership profile. • Identify friends and relatives of members not presently in the church.
4. SELECT TARGET COMMUNITIES	• Recognize the people groups who will best fit into your church.
5. PRIORITIZE THE TARGET COMMUNITIES	• Identify available resources within the church and allocate them to the most potentially productive areas.
6. DEVELOP SPECIFIC STRATEGIES FOR REACHING EACH COMMUNITY	• Use gifts, strengths, special interests of lay members. • Identify needs the church can effectively meet.

Used with permission.

strategic steps outlined in the above chart developed by the American Institute of Church Growth.

CLASSES AND CLASSIFICATIONS

Socio-economic status (SES) is a fundamental variable in market analysis. Some believe it is a better predictor of attitudes and consumer behavior patterns than any other single factor. One social scientist says,

Studies of social class in the several regions of the United States demonstrate that it is a major determinant of individual decisions and social actions and that every area of economic life is directly and

189

indirectly influenced by our class order and that the major decisions of most individuals are partly controlled by it.[11]

Social class is usually indicated by factors like income, occupation, housing, and education, but may also include some particular perspectives on life.

A recent article, "How to Be Class Conscious," defines people simply as "upscalers" or "downscalers." The "upscale" class are typically oriented to achievement in their work and "consider their occupation the single most important source of their personal identification."[12] When asked who they are, they are likely to tell you what they *do*. On the other hand, the "downscale" class are more typically oriented to security in their work. When asked who they are, I suspect they are more than likely to tell you where they come from. A traditional description of social classes might also be listed as upper-class (wealthy elite), lower upper-class (high-income professionals), upper middle-class (educated professionals), lower middle-class (typical hardworking Americans), upper lower-class (average workers), and lower lower-class (poverty level).

Another popular way to position people is in "blue-collar" or "white-collar" professions. Between the early twentieth-century Industrial Age and the coming twenty-first-century Information Age in America, blue-collar occupations will decline from over 60 percent to less than 30 percent of the work force. Out of a total of 40 million new jobs in the past twenty-five years, only 3 million were in manufacturing industries, although other blue-collar jobs like those in the home industries have increased. Some large blue-collar churches have pastors whose management styles are like "foremen," with mechanized methods of ministry, such as Jack Hyles in industrial Hammond, Indiana. In a recent book on *Blue Collar Ministry,* author-pastor Tex Sample found that a principle of "reciprocity" and the exchange of favors, as well as the pastor's ability to "play" with his people, were essential ingredients for his effectiveness in a smaller church. He says blue-collar churches stress belonging more than upper middle-class values like achievement. Because life-styles and values are different, he concludes that a typical middle-class ministry will not be effective in a blue-collar community.

White-collar vocations have historically been filled by both middle- and upper-class people. Some social analysts see a trend that the mass market of the middle-class, however, is splitting apart. According to *Fortune* magazine, "The so-called upscale market is growing rapidly—by 1990 about one-third of personal income will be received by households with incomes of $50,000 or more . . . the class market will become a mass market."[13]

Recently, a new designation has been coined: "gold-collar" professions. This new breed of intelligent, interdependent, and innovative workers will major on brain power, not brawn, and they will soon represent 60 percent of the work force. In terms of management styles, these well-educated professionals probably won't respond as well to older, industrial-era values like autocracy, homogeneity, and loyalty. They will want to replace bureaucratic models with ones that affirm values like democracy, pluralism, and creative thinking. With new business buzzwords like *entrepreneurship, intrepreneurship,* and *personal self-management,* "it becomes evident that gold-collar workers and society are closely aligned, whereas traditional management values and practices are quite different."[14] This new pursuit of what is called "Managerial Empowerment" for the twenty-first century will have implications for the management and marketing strategies of churches that minister-managers will need to reflect upon.

Any attempt to analyze the white-collar, or upcoming

gold-collar work force soon reveals that very distinctive sets of characteristics can also be classified and targeted for ministry. For example, one major marketing firm offers "Prism Target Marketing," which can identify market segments of life-style clusters by zip codes and census neighborhoods. One cluster group would be "urban gold coast" dwellers (singles, couples, few children) who are at least college-educated and who live in upscale, multi-unit (usually high-rise) housing. At Moody Church, we commissioned a group with our singles pastor to begin a new contemporary church in Chicago that will target this segment of our ministry-market.

Another major marketing firm provides information to target the "affluent market," which identifies prime neighborhoods of people who earn more than $40,000 per year. At Moody Church we established a monthly business club luncheon at downtown Marshall Field's to target this type of "upscale" market. Our first major evangelistic event prior to that was a first-class executive dinner at the Chicago Arts Club, where over one-hundred nonchurch people heard the gospel through a professional's testimony. Some people were saved! The most recent evangelistic event was to rent a yacht for an evening dinner cruise on Lake Michigan, where many couples heard the story of a successful man who found Christ.

Some churches have been quite successful in targeting an "upscale" market. In New England, where there are too few large evangelical churches, two examples come to mind. One of them is Grace Chapel in Lexington, Massachusetts, which grew from 400 to 3,000 in a decade. This somewhat eclectic but strong evangelical church is located near the high-tech corridor of Route 138 outside Boston. It has attracted many management and technical professionals who are oriented to achievement and operate with corporate mind-sets for management in the church. Another example is the Community Baptist Church in Avon, Connecticut, a businessmen's bedroom community for Hartford. This church started about a decade ago and now has over five-hundred members, with plans to be a two-thousand member regional church in another decade or two. Unlike a lot of other rural, small town, blue-collar or lower middle-class churches in New England, these professional, goal-oriented people have attracted others to Christ and their growing churches.

Having completed this simple but extended introduction into the sophisticated world of target marketing for ministry, it is obvious there is much more expertise to explore than I have been able to expound upon. Only in the last decade or so have nonprofit organizations such as hospitals and schools attempted to apply marketing concepts. In the process they have discovered the translation of marketing moxie into their terms has been much more complex than originally thought. At least two distinctives often create this difficulty. One is that nonprofit voluntary organizations frequently face pressure not to pick out a market segment if it leads to ignoring other main groups. The other is that they often have mission mandates that make demands conflicting with the desires of their market. MADD (Mothers Against Drunk Driving), for example, targets people who basically do not want to change their conduct.

Similar problems can confront the church, but intentional marketing to target groups can prove very effective. Peter Wagner's fifth "vital sign" of a healthy church is that it draws its membership primarily (though not exclusively) from a homogeneous group. In the study of 425 fastest growing Southern Baptist churches previously referred to, most of the churches were formed primarily along homogeneous lines, and the top fifteen had a preponderance of membership coming from similar types of employment. The natural networks for life-style evangelism have more potential in these churches. In regards to his ministry, Paul said that he was "under obligation both to Greeks and to barbarians, both to the wise and to the foolish" (Rom. 1:14). While the church at large should have a similar agenda, the local church might do well to "target-market" its ministry for maximum effectiveness. In the process, two theological assumptions may make marketing more acceptable to church people who feel they should love everyone in general and not one group in particular.

The first theological assumption we must make is that people's fundamental need of Christ is universal and the message of the Cross is absolute. We must preach repentance and faith in Jesus Christ (Luke 24:44; Acts 20:20). The second theological assumption is that people's felt need of Christ is individual and the ministry of the church is therefore adaptable. The Lord Jesus responded differently to Nicodemus (John 3) who knew the Scriptures and showed a spiritual interest in Him than He did to the woman at the well (John 4), who came from a different perspective. As marketing consultant Jim Engel says, "The goal is not to *make* the gospel relevant but rather to communicate the relevance of the gospel. . . . In communicating gospel relevance, felt need is taken as a starting point."[15] As Sandu Singh once said about missions, "We have to give the water of life in an Indian cup!"

For example, at the 1987 Super Bowl game in Pasadena a highly committed Christian, dressed in a three-piece suit, greeted people going to the game dressed in cut-offs and casual clothes. He raised a placard saying, "Repent!" Surely it would have been more effective if an equally courageous Christian dressed in Calvin Klein jeans, a Ralph Lauren polo shirt, designer sunglasses and topsiders carried a professional ad sign that said, "Ask me about living forever." As another example, I am currently talking with a Christian publisher about producing a series of videocassette programs to be used in homes for ultimate evangelistic purposes, but which would also meet the felt needs of both Christians and non-Christians. Some of the titles might be "Stress Management for the Single Parent" or "How to Survive the Singles Scene." Prepared with a simple discussion guide (and maybe a resource book), this would give Christians who are not talented teachers a tool to practice life-style evangelism outside the church, or even inside the church, to target special small groups.

There is a trend toward the development of a well-educated, upscale, gold-collar professional market—people that are younger, secular, and unchurched. This group might be typified by the yuppie segment of the market—people who represent only 6 percent of the population but who are style-setters for others. *Newsweek* called 1984 "the Year of the Yuppie." A whole new vocabulary developed from this designation:

1. Yumpies—young upwardly mobile professionals
2. Guppies—graying or aging urban professionals
3. Buppies—black urban professionals
4. Yummies—yuppie mommies
5. Dinks—yuppies with double incomes and no children, and
6. Podwags—parents of dinks who are eagerly awaiting their grandchildren to be born.

A new set of "status symbols" has also developed which includes a BMW, VCR, personal computer, health club membership, gourmet foods, and, more recently, the Filofax, which is a book-sized personal organizer with phone numbers, wine lists, world maps, and the basics of a portable mini-office. A *Yuppie Handbook* has also been published for this group.

Geographically, more yuppies are now living in the

suburbs where they grew up than in the city centers. Sociologically, more of them are beginning to have families and will be concerned about the education of their children. Economically, they are upwardly mobile in their life-style and very transient in their careers. Spiritually, they are hard to reach. Because many of these baby boomer yuppies are well-educated, they take Christianity less seriously.

According to Jim Reapsome's analysis of baby boomers, two things confirm this: (1) "A college education doesn't do much for one's religious faith: in fact, Americans with only a grade school education are more consistently religious in belief and practice than those who have been to college."[16] As a group, college-educated persons rank lower in belief of God. (2) Older people hold more to Christian ethics or beliefs than do younger people. Another observation made by Chuck Colson is (3) that "the yuppies are apparently convinced that money is the root of all good."[17] (They are also self-serving politically.) However, I read recently about a book entitled *Modern Madness: The Emotional Fallout of Success,* in which a Washington, D.C., psychologist says many yuppies are unhappy. In addition, the Stanford Business School says that in the business world we may soon see the biggest wave of midcareer crises we have ever seen. Yuppies are finding that the fast lane sometimes leads to a dead end. In some respects, they are a restless generation.

I would like to share one outstanding example of a church that has successfully reached yuppies as well as a broad range of professional suburbanites who live near affluent South Barrington, Illinois. The church, now located on 110 acres of land, started about eleven years ago in a theater and is called Willow Creek Community Church. It currently has two Sunday morning services for over twelve-thousand people, and they have just begun a Saturday night service as well. I have been told it is one of the three fastest growing churches in America. The founder-pastor of the church is Bill Hybels. He is in his mid-thirties, and as the son of a very successful Christian businessman he is very attuned to the affluent market. He says, "We have thousands of young professionals in our church, and they have learned that trying to find fulfillment in life through acquiring material acquisitions is like chasing the wind—it just won't do it." How this model of ministry has been developed is really a case study in target marketing.

Based upon a taped message, my own visits to the church, and some discussion with the pastor, the following seven-point summary shows the unique strategy of ministry they have developed. Their target market is "Unchurched Harry," envisioned as sitting in his suburban subdivision home on Sunday morning, watching TV or reading a newspaper, but unattracted to church or the Christian faith and life-style. Their seven-point strategy is geared to reaching that man and bringing him to Christ (Col. 1:27).

(1) Because "Unchurched Harry" and his wife, "Unchurched Mary," are totally isolated from real Christianity, the primary point of entry into their lives must be bridges that believers can build with them through personal relationships. Willow Creek is committed to "life-style evangelism" throughout the church staff and ministry and especially through the laity.

(2) As a redemptive relationship is being established, believers are encouraged to pray for opportunities to share a verbal witness as well (Rom. 10:17).

(3) As a supplement to life-style evangelism in the marketplace, the church provides a uniquely designed Sunday morning service primarily for "seekers." Earlier in his ministry Bill surveyed people to find out why they do not attend church. The main objections were that churches always ask for money and church services are often boring. To meet the first objection, they tell

guests they are not expected to give. To meet the second objection, they provide a nontraditional service.

The setting for the service is a large auditorium with a stage, no religious symbols, and windows along the side to view their grounds. The style of their service is contemporary. Congregational singing includes a worship chorus printed in the bulletin. Special music is provided by talented singers utilizing contemporary repertoire and backed by a full orchestra or band of young musicians using piano, drums, synthesizer, electric guitars, and brass. The Scripture reading is introduced by a contemporary context or story that fits the text. The church often provides multimedia or slide shows and always puts on a brief dramatic presentation to illustrate the thematic focus of the service. The sermons, though very applicable to Christians at large, are geared toward seekers who know very little Scripture. Bill sometimes calls his messages "Christianity 101."

This nontraditional, nonthreatening format where Christians can bring non-Christians is based on four basic assumptions about "seekers": (a) The seeker initially wants anonymity. They don't want to sing anything, sign anything, say anything, or give anything. (b) The seeker needs introductory Christian "milk" rather than "meat" (1 Cor. 3). (c) The seeker will respond to relevant, life-oriented messages based on the Bible. (d) The seeker has expectations of excellence. So the staff reviews every service to do "quality control" for Christ's sake.

The next four steps are simple to review. The next step (4) is to attend the Wednesday night "New Community" worship service for believers. The process of assimilation into this sphere of church life is expected to be through the personal tug of a trusted Christian friend. The next two steps (5 and 6) are invitation and induction into small groups and Christian service. The final goal of this process (7) is spiritual reproduction, when former "Unchurched Harry" and his wife reach out to "Unchurched Larry." Some observers are saying Willow Creek is the model for the twenty-first-century church. For many situations that are similar, this may be true. Too many churches are isolated from unchurched people and are not attractive to them. But Pastor Hybels simply says it is a model that the Holy Spirit has given them for their situation and that's one main reason it works so well. Certainly the surge in secularism should cause many traditional churches to rethink their strategy for ministry.

To be more effective, a minister-manager needs to not only utilize an appropriate "style-flex" for management but also a "style-flex" for ministry that is appropriate to the particular situation. Simply summarized, this involves a *market analysis* of the church and community, a *marketing audit* to discover what the "match factors" are between the church and community or between the strengths of the church and some special groups in the community. And last, but not least, a *market aim* where you determine who your church is reaching and/or which distinct market your ministry should be designed for. This leads us then to the next topic in our typology of management, which I call "sight," more commonly referred to as vision.

NOTES

1. Kent R. Hunter, *Your Church Has Personality* (Nashville: Abingdon, 1985), 22.
2. Daniel R. Reeves and Ronald Jenson, *Always Advancing: Modern Strategies for Church Growth* (San Bernardino, Calif.: Here's Life, 1984), 91.
3. Edgar H. Schein, "What You Need to Know About Organizational Culture," *Training and Development Journal* 38, January 1984, 30-33.
4. Stanley M. Davis, *Managing Corporate Culture* (Cambridge, Mass.: Ballinger, 1984), 6-8.
5. George W. Bullard, Jr., "An Analysis of Change in Selected Southern Baptist Churches in Metropolitan Transitional Areas, 1965-1975," Home Missions Board, Southern Baptist Convention, 3.

6. Douglas Walrath, "Why Some Churches Thrive . . . and Others Don't," *Action Information* (The Alban Institute, Inc., 4125 Nebraska Avenue, NW, Washington, DC 20016), November 1978, 13.
7. C. Peter Wagner, *Leading Your Church to Growth* (Ventura, Calif.: Regal, 1984), 174-175.
8. Montgomery Smith, "Homogeneity and American Church Growth: A Case Study" (Ph.D. diss., Fuller Theological Seminary, 1976), 249.
9. Paul Chance, "The One Who Has the Most Toys When He Dies, Wins," *Psychology Today,* May 1987, 54.
10. Marshall Shelley, "Home Visitation: How Well Does It Work?" *Leadership,* Spring 1984, 81.
11. Sidney J. Levy, *Marketplace Behavior: It's Meaning for Management* (New York: AMACOM, a division of the American Management Associations, 1978), 119.
12. Robert B. Settle and Pamela Alreck, "How to Be Class Conscious," *Success,* June 1987, 8
13. Bruce Steinberg, "The Mass Market Is Splitting Apart," *Fortune,* 28 November 1983, 82.
14. Robert F. Kelley, *The Gold Collar Worker: Harvesting the Brain Power of the New Workforce* (Reading, Mass.: Addison-Wesley, 1985), 35.
15. James F. Engel, *Contemporary Christian Communication* (Nashville: Thomas Nelson, 1979), 318.
16. James W. Reapsome, "Religious Values: Reflection of Age and Education," *Christianity Today,* 2 May 1980, 24.
17. Charles W. Colson, "A Call to Rescue the Yuppies," *Christianity Today,* 17 May 1985, 18.

TEN

SEEING VISIONS, DREAMING DREAMS:

SIGHT AND MANAGEMENT

In 1973, an American Management Association study of six-thousand American managers and company presidents revealed that the two chief causes of ineffective executive productivity were (1) a lack of well-defined goals and objectives and (2) inadequate managerial leadership. A decade later, *Fortune* magazine reported that executive recruiters were being asked to find corporate candidates with two primary qualifications for effective leadership: (1) *vision,* which involves the ability to make clear the special purpose of the organization, and (2) *charisma,* which involves the ability to motivate people to produce in the organization. Leaders and managers in many fields today are expected to exhibit a special ability to see clearly the vision, purpose, mission, or goals an organization or group should focus on for its future.

In politics, consider the impact on American civil rights when Martin Luther King, Jr., said he had seen the promised land and told his people, "I have a dream!" Today there are black rock groups that draw black and white crowds for concerts and feel they are in some sense fulfilling Dr. King's dream for America. In psychology success motivation seminars and PMA (Positive Mental Attitude) workshops are teaching the techniques of creative visualization and goal setting. Their speakers claim that the use of the mind's inherent "dream machine" has been a distinguishing characteristic of high achievers. Management psychologist Warren Bennis studied ninety top leaders and discovered that one common characteristic among them was the compelling vision and dreams they had about their work. Even average Americans have been inspired to fulfill their personal destiny if they will simply "dream the impossible dream." The words of *Alice in Wonderland* are applicable today to both managers and ministers alike: "If you don't know where you are going, any road will get you there." It's one thing to know how to build a road to get somewhere—it's another thing to know where the road should go. In terms of today's leadership theory effective leaders see the right things to do, while managers are efficient in seeing to it that those things are done right.

Most ministers are familiar with the statement in Acts 2:17 that in the last days God would pour forth His Spirit so that young men would see visions and old men would dream dreams. The biblical focus of these visions (e.g., John in Revelation) or dreams (e.g., Joseph in Genesis) include God's person and His attributes, His perspective and His absolutes, and His purposes and His anticipation of the future. Biblical prophets were both forth-tellers of God's truth as well as fore-tellers of God's plans.

Immediately we can think of biblical models who were visionaries under God: Noah, Abraham, Moses, Caleb, and a host of others who made it to God's "Hall of Fame" by faith (Heb. 11). Men and women of God today can also have visions and dreams that have been conceived and constructed by the Lord Jesus Christ who is the real Author and Finisher of our faith

(Heb. 12:1–2). How these truths may be translated into twentieth-century management terms and techniques for the minister-manager is the subject of this chapter.

IDEAS ABOUT VISIONS AND DREAMS

Visions and dreams, in the contemporary context of the corporate world and church life, are sometimes initiated through one person and sometimes through other processes. Leaders with different styles of management in different situations may utilize at least four ideas of this concept.

Visionary Leadership. Some individual leaders have a special ability to conceive and create the visions, dreams, mission, or goals by which an organization should set its future agenda. It has been found in some studies that these leaders are often good listeners and that the way in which they conceptualize a vision is through their own personal investigation of a situation. When Nehemiah heard that Jerusalem was in disrepair, he made an on-site tour. He wrote, "I arose in the night, I and a few men with me. I did not tell anyone what my God was putting into my mind to do for Jersualem. . . . So I went out at night . . . inspecting the walls" (Neh. 2:12-13). God gave him a purpose to pursue, and after reviewing the situation, he developed a plan to accomplish that purpose. It reminds me of *A Passion for Excellence* which discusses MBWA: Management by Walking Around. It says, "We believe in truly listening to the customer . . . we believe in truly listening to our people."[1] Proverbs 18:15 says, "The intelligent man is always open to new ideas. In fact, he looks for them" (TLB). A vision or dream may be fuzzy at first, but when it's focused by "being in touch" with the situation, it can be clarified and conceptualized by people who are visionary leaders.

Leaders: The Strategies for Taking Charge says that vision is the first most important strategy.

> To choose a direction, a leader must have first developed a mental image of a possible and desirable future state of the organization. This image, which we call a vision, may be as vague as a dream or as precise as a goal or a mission statement. The critical point is that the vision articulates a view of a realistic, credible, attractive future for the organization, a condition that is better in some important ways than what now exists.[2]

Leaders have the ability to select, synthesize, and articulate the appropriate vision. Once this vision has been made known through models, mottos, metaphors, or mission statements, it must be incorporated into the organization's culture, reinforced through strategic planning and decision making, and implemented through appropriate motivation or "charisma."

In another book entitled *Creating Excellence,* the authors make an observation that is applicable to church life: "If we had to choose one essential characteristic of what we call the New Age, it would be change . . . only those leaders who learn to anticipate and invent the future will profit from, rather than be surprised by, change."[3] In the chapter "Vision: Creating the Future," they describe the visionary executive as a skillful strategic player who (a) articulates philosophy and (b) talks about future goals, though he also (c) makes contact with people and (d) is expressive and supportive to them. Their definition of a vision is "a mental journey from the known to the unknown, creating a future from a montage of current facts, hopes, dreams, dangers, and opportunities."[4] Pastors should read both of these books for greater insights on the idea of visionary leaders.

Mission Statements. In his 1954 book, *The Practice of Management,* Peter Drucker made the point that the first responsibility of the manager was to know the mission of his company. Three decades later, in *In Search of Excellence,* Peters and Waterman said effective corporate executives were also able to articulate their company purpose or goals in a succinct statement that would focus the energy of the organization. This so-called trendy concept has developed a "mission mania"; three-fourths of the Fortune 500 companies now have official mission statements. Many other companies have concentrated on the concept of corporate culture and have also developed similar statements that state the basic values to be used to guide their organization into the future. Bob Townsend, author of *Up the Organization,* took six months to develop a twenty-three-word statement that helped revitalize Avis as a multi-million-dollar company. He said, "We want to become the fastest growing company with the highest profit margins in the business of renting and leasing vehicles without drivers."

In a recent article, Mark Roman makes the point that setting the vision in words is the crucial executive act. He says the mission statement is a proclamation of corporate purpose and the single most important driving force of the organization. It may appear in public as a slogan (e.g., "We Try Harder" or "We Are a Church That Cares"), but it is more often a few dozen well-chosen words that identify the market and the mission of that organization. Two of his comments are critical in their application to the church. One is that a mission statement is only as effective as the executive (or minister-manager) who pens it. The second is that most organizations have a natural entropy when individuals within the company develop too many different ideas as to what the company should do. He says, "It's the leader's job to keep that from happening and get the people thinking along the same line. Mission statements help channel the energy of everyone in the same direction."[5] They can also act as a springboard for necessary structural changes.

There are at least three reasons why a corporate vision or mission statement may be difficult for a church to define. The first of these may be the infusion of new members into the church. While new ideas and insights may enhance an organizational focus and bring revitalization to a church, they may also entangle it. I had breakfast recently with the associate executive pastor of a very large church that has a well-defined plan. He said, "We have a stranglehold on our philosophy of ministry. It is nonnegotiable!" The flip side of fresh ideas may be frustration when there is no clear united corporate church strategy. A second difficulty may be a democratic process of church management by which leadership can't define an overall purpose because too many members want to debate it. A third difficulty may arise if there has been too much decentralization. If a church has sincerely decided to foster independent development of organizations or departments, or by reason of default, has simply allowed them (e.g., adult Sunday school classes), it may have a mutiny on its hands if the church attempts a new strategy and/or structural direction for the ministry. The sensitive subject of blending individual and institutional goals is a subject minister-managers will need to study further than this chapter can fully discuss.

Some church mission statements are biblical but too broad or too bland. The Institute for American Church Growth believes a mission statement is crucial. They suggest that there are five components necessary for a good statement:

1. A biblical understanding of what you believe is God's special mission for your church

2. A geographic area for ministry
3. A target audience of people you intend to focus on
4. A list of activities you plan for outreach
5. The expected results.

Church mission statements with these components can be used in the next process which some churches use in directing their ministry.

Strategic Planning. The abilities of visionary leadership and those of strategic planning are not always equally found in one executive or minister-manager. General George Patton was a visionary leader, while General Omar Bradley was a strategic planner. Some authors advocate that a vision (or even a mission statement) should answer the question of *what* the purpose of the organization is, while planning addresses the question of *how* the purpose will be accomplished. As we have seen, some definitions of leadership and management (i.e., doing the right things and doing things right) are compatible with the comments of Ted Engstrom when he says that

> dreams and visions usually come to one person. Plans, on the other hand, are the result of corporate planning. . . . Dreams and visions are intuitive . . . plans are very rational . . . . The difference between a rational thinker and an intuitive thinker is that the rational thinker can explain the process.[6]

This raises two questions, the first of which is *who* should do the strategic planning? Depending on the style of the minister-manager and the situation of the ministry, there are at least four options that may be selected for strategic planning: (1) the pastoral staff and/ or church board in concert with a selected leader, (2) a planning committee that will make recommendations for official decisions, (3) a special planning committee that will develop the resources and processes by which the planning process will be pursued, or (4) an outside consultant or consulting team equipped to explore objectively the possibilities with the leadership group.

The second question is in regards to *what* may be involved in the planning process. One model that might be helpful is found in *Strategic Planning for Church Organizations* by Richard Broholm. He says there are four very basic elements in the process. First of all, *assumptions* must be analyzed regarding the theological, environmental, and operational values that underlie the ministry. These set the intellectual boundaries for realistic strategic thinking. Next come the *objectives* (or goals), which are simple statements of the targets to be reached (including dates). It answers the question, What? The purpose statement answers the question, Why? The next element is *strategy,* the methods that will be chosen to accomplish the purpose and goals. This answers the question, How? The last element is *tactics,* the specific steps that will be taken to implement the strategy. This also often answers the question, Who? He also advises two important guidelines: (1) "a structure and method for regular review and evaluation is essential to the strategic-planning process," and (2) "it is important to build in a discipline of accountability right from the beginning."[7] As I have already noted, a good situational analysis often precedes a good strategic planning process.

Goal Setting. By definition, organizational theory assumes that all organizations exist for some purpose, mission, or overarching goal. Church responses to goal setting vary, but in the corporate world, research has shown that goal-driven individuals and institutions usually produce greater achievements. One management seminar leader says that only 5 percent of our nation's business leaders understand and utilize the latest and most effective goal-setting techniques. There is a natural tendency in some managers to avoid specifically stated goals or objectives because they are more accountable in the case of failure. I also suspect the same reluctance can be found in church leaders for the same reasons.

On the other hand, sometimes the reluctance is to avoid man-made goals for which we hold God accountable. Pastor Jack Hayford of the Church on the Way in California has seen his church grow from fifty to over five-thousand in fifteen years. In an article entitled "Why I Don't Set Goals," he expresses his concern that goals are not his, but God's. He says we should ask two fundamental questions about church goal-setting: (1) Is this goal a direct result of a God-given directive? and (2) Does this goal sacrifice any principle or people on the altar of expediency?[8] His concern is not to "plan a birth" but to let God "birth a plan."

Many goals are appropriate for strategic planning, but a major concern for a church should be growth goals. Most church growth leaders stress the importance of numerically measurable evangelistic goals. It seems plain enough in the Bible that Luke, author of Acts, thought it was important to count the numbers (if not the individual names) of people who were converted to Christ in the early church (Acts 2:40, 47). Some would argue that we should only be faithful to God, and He will decide how fruitful we should be. While there is truth to this, the point can also be made through many case studies that good goals can be God's goals for growth to make us more fruitful. Good goals should have at least the following four characteristics: suitability, measurability, achievability, and accountability. Even though some would argue against goal setting in the church, it is very widely used with different techniques for individual or institutional pursuits.

INDIVIDUALS WITH VISIONS AND DREAMS

In 1976 Henry Mintzberg analyzed leadership thinking styles and made two interesting observations. First, he suggested that

> an organization will rely largely on one individual to conceptualize its strategy, to synthesize a "vision" of how the organization will respond to its environment. In other words: scratch an interesting strategy, and you will probably find a single strategy formulator beneath it. Creative, integrated strategies seem to be the product of single brains.[9]

Second, he suggested that executive policy-makers are usually more intuitive than intellectual in their approach to leadership challenges. In 1984 Daniel J. Isenberg also analyzed the thinking processes of a dozen executives and found that they were similar in that they sometimes ignored the implied linear progression of rational decision making and relied more on intuitive thinking. In practice he found that "executives work on an issue until they find a match between their 'gut' and their 'head.' "[10] Senior managers demonstrated they had developed very perceptive, intuitive thinking styles.

Both of these *Harvard Business Review* articles illustrate distinctions between "leaders" and "managers" described in chapter 2. They also emphasize that leaders are often characterized by more intuitive-innovative styles of thinking. This basic perspective has been more recently refined and articulated in the excellent book *Corporate Pathfinders: How Visionary Managers Use Imaginative Strategies to Shape the Future of Their Companies.* The book's thesis is that total management process involves three phases. The first is pathfinding, which involves mission, purpose and a vision, or the *aim* of an organization. The second is problem-solving, which involves planning and rational decision-making processes, or the *analysis* of an organization. The third is implementing, which involves doing and influencing others to do, or the *action* of an organization.

The second part of the thesis is that individual managers operate in all three dimensions of the management process, but they usually major on one predominant style. Some leaders are primarily pathfinders to point the way, others are problem-solvers to plan the way, and still others are people-movers to get others to go that way. Some leaders are capable of both the qualities looked for in executive searches: vision and charisma. The third part of the thesis is that in the past two decades education has concentrated on problem-solving skills. Now we need a new emphasis on pathfinder skills. (Look in a bookstore and you will find titles like *The Intuitive Manager.*)

Harold Leavitt, author of *Corporate Pathfinders,* says,

> The pathfinders of the world show at least three important and distinguishable attributes: they are men and women of visions; their value systems are clear, and strongly held; and they are determined to turn their vision into realities.[11]

How managers and ministers may become personal pathfinders can be better understood by considering four current concepts that are often considered in the development of "visions and dreams."

Creative Intelligence. In 1981 neurosurgeon Robert Sperry won the Nobel Prize in medicine for his development of left brain-right brain hemispheric psychology, sometimes called brain dominance theory. Simply stated, each brain sphere is presumed to produce distinctive functions and thinking abilities, one of which is creative intelligence.

His studies and others are said to indicate that "left-brain" people tend to think sequentially, while "right-brain" people tend to think synonymously. The result is the difference between a rational approach to management and a creative approach to management. "Left-brain" managers are said to be intellectual. They prefer solving problems by breaking them down into parts. They use the "hard facts" of logic and data, are verbally oriented, are structured in their approach, and usually prefer authoritative systems. On the other hand, "right-brain" managers are imaginative. They approach problems through their intuition, utilize the "soft facts" of impressions, are visually oriented, more spontaneous, and prefer participatory systems.

On the assumption that brain dominance theory is correct, many authors today advocate the development of these neglected "right-brain" qualities. Books like *Whole Brain Thinking* say we can learn to use both sides of the brain to achieve peak job performance. One brain specialist has developed a Whole Brain Corporation to train executives in creativity.

Some have challenged this point of view as simplistic, saying, "None of this left brain-right brain 'mythology' is supported by actual research. . . . What has been thought to be a dichotomy of function between the hemispheres turns out to be a gradient of abilities. . . . These differences are of degree, not of type."[12] Since then, the *New York Times* has reported that each hemisphere can, in fact, perform the function of the other. The *Chicago Tribune* has also reported one psychologist as saying that any truly creative production really requires an integration of both brain hemispheres.

Still, there is no doubt that many writers are taking this theory seriously. In *The Gold Collar Worker,* there is a chapter on the need for "Cultivating Brainpower" in the future because "the U.S. educational system tends to ignore right brain development, whereas popular entertainment forms, such as movies and computer games, bombard it."[13] In the book *Re-inventing the Corporation,* John Naisbett contrasts an Industrial Age educational paradigm, which stressed values of uniformity, control, and centralization with the need for a new Information Age educational paradigm that can deal with rapid change in a "data-drenched" world. His discussion of TLC (Thinking, Learning, and Creating) argues that managers of the future should learn new abilities like "imagineering" to cope with the coming challenges. These observations suggest that natural creative intelligence can and should be enhanced. (We should also remember the comment of Thomas Edison, who said, "Invention is ninety-nine percent perspiration and one percent inspiration." Thinking is work.)

Creative Visualization. One of the top trends today in psychology and education, this concept has captured the imagination of leaders in all walks of life. By definition, this process moves the future into the present by what Norman Vincent Peale calls "positive imaging." Others call it "mental movies," and some call it "mind-zapping." The idea is that if you are able to formulate an idea or plan, build a clear picture of it with your imagination, and can state it in terms that others can see as well, you will successfully create your vision's fulfillment. Expectations affect attitudes, which affect actions, which then affect achievement. Success Motivation seminars teach the techniques of imaging in goal setting, and audiocassette programs on the new neuropsychology of achievement discuss the power of three-dimensional visualization and the internalization of your achievement image. New books, like *Wishcraft: Pinpoint Your Goals and Make Your Dreams Come True* and *Imagineering: How to Profit from Your Creative Powers* are luring many into a mental journey that promises success.

Promises of success, achievement, and personal fulfillment make the idea of creative visualization attractive popular psychology. However practical some of these psychological principles may prove to be, the Christian needs a word of caution regarding the ideology that underlines much of the terminology. Consider these three comparisons of statements from secular and spiritual sources on the subject.

In *Creative Visualization* we are told that what we can conceive, and believe, we will achieve. The source of this fulfillment in this New Age movement is simply *something* higher, "call it what you will," the laws of nature, or even God within you. But the Christian's faith is in Someone Higher, the Lord Jesus. (I do not believe in the positive confession theology of those who say, "Just name it and claim it.")

In *The Miracle of Sports Psychology* the author says that even though we know a goal may be in the future, "Successful mental programming requires that it be stated as a present tense, already recognized fact."[14] Whatever we vividly imagine, ardently desire, sincerely believe, and enthusiastically act upon *must* come to pass. The Bible defines faith in Hebrews 11 as "the substance of things hoped for, the evidence of things not seen. The secular view is that the mind's "dream machine" will create the means for a subconscious fulfillment of the vision that is clearly imagined as being fulfilled. The scriptural view is that faith is rooted and grounded in God's Word and will be fulfilled by His Spirit, according to His will.

Another advocate of creative visualization says, "The man who expects great things, makes noble plans, and daily pursues them cannot help but succeed." Consider the famous words of William Carey by comparison: "Expect great things from God; attempt great things for God." The secular source of creative visualization is human potential. For the Christian, it is heaven's potential that we seek to "supply all of our needs" (Phil. 4:19).

When he considers the fact that visualization has been used by psychic healers, tantric Yoga, Christian Science, ancient Egyptian followers of Hermes, occult practice, and now the New Age movement, the minister-manager must make a discerning judgment of this phenomenon even when it appears in management literature and in motivational seminars. Christian author Dave Hunt says the "supreme secret" of this movement is in reality a "counterfeit faith."[15]

The Gift of Faith. According to the Scriptures, Christians are not only saved by faith (Eph. 2:8-9), we are also called to serve by faith (Gal. 2:20). This faith is capable of growth (Luke 17:5) and may be considered "little faith" (Matt. 14:31) or "great faith" (Matt. 8:10) by God. Studies show that faith, leadership, and goal setting are often involved in the attitudes and accomplishments of growing churches. A few years ago, a report of some growing churches in California concluded that a very important factor in their growth was the faith of its leadership. Harold Fickett led the First Baptist Church of Van Nuys, California, to a membership of over seventeen-thousand in the early seventies. In his book, *Hope for Your Church*, he said,

> There are many contributing factors to our growth. But the one thing from the human standpoint that is above all others is the fact that laymen of our church really believe that with God all things are

possible, and they are willing to act upon this faith.[16]

Some minister-managers also have the special gift of faith (1 Cor. 12:9). As I have already noted, Peter Wagner says church growth pastors have this gift along with the gift of leadership (Rom. 12:8). The gift of faith enables them to know where to go, while the gift of leadership enables them to know how to get there or how to get others to go with them. We can see here that faith is the equivalent of the "vision" leaders need today, and leadership is the equivalent of "charisma." Peter Wagner says the gift of faith is "the special ability to discern with extraordinary confidence the will and purpose of God and the future of the work."[17] Even though Wagner and Towns found all superchurch pastors possess these gifts, I would also add that since gifts are given in degree, many other pastors and church workers can also exhibit these gifts in their own ministries.

How does one identify the "gift of faith"? In my first church after seminary, three months after arriving, I had a "vision" for our church to start another church in a smaller community nearby. I was led to announce this vision at my first watch-night service with them, and five years later we started the other church, which is still ministering today. What this a "gift" of faith or an expression of "good" faith that God honored? The Bible talks about the "grace" of giving (2 Cor. 8–9), but it also talks about a "gift" of giving (Rom. 12:7). Sometimes it is difficult to discern which is operative. The same is true of faith.

In their book *Stepping Out on Faith,* Jerry Falwell and Elmer Towns provide the interested minister-manager with an in-depth discussion of the subject, as well as a demonstration of this gift in the lives of ten pastors. They provide a survey of three definitions. (1) An *in-*

strumental view of faith is the ability to use the promises of God's Word (Eph. 6:16) to live the Christian life.
(2) An *insightful* view of faith is "a Spirit-given ability to
see something that God wants done and to sustain un-
wavering confidence that God will do it, regardless of
seemingly insurmountable obstacles.[18] In this view,
God activates the vision, but it is through the one having the vision that it is accomplished. These leaders are
usually (a) growth-oriented, (b) goal-directed, (c) optimistic, and (d) confident. (3) The *interventional* view
may be called a "miracle-working faith" or "wonder-
working faith," and it involves prayer that God will in-
tervene in a situation to overcome problems and
change circumstances. This most thorough discussion
of the subject says "even though there seem to be three
different ways that the gift of faith is interpreted . . . the
authors believe that these three definitions are three
cumulative steps in exercising the gifts of faith.[19] If we
focus in on definition two, the minister-manager desir-
ing church growth may pray for the "gift of faith," or
simply for greater faith, to accomplish His will. One of
the ways this prayer could be answered is through the
setting of goals.

The Goals of Faith. Another avenue of church growth
leadership is the setting of goals by the pastor. Now it is
true that many good churches grow without numerical
evangelistic goals. A study was done some years ago of
churches pastored by David Hocking, John MacArthur,
Gene Getz, Bill Yaeger, Ray Ortlund, and Joe Aldrich.
None of these were characterized by church growth
goals, but they were led by men who had proven leadership abilities and strong philosophies of ministry. On
the other hand, many churches have seen greater
growth when their pastors have stepped out in faith to
believe God for greater results.

One model for this is the Church Growth Workshop, which was initiated by missionary Vergil Gerber on the Venezuelan mission field in 1972. He gathered forty-seven pastors, missionaries, and church leaders for four days of study, prayer, and the establishment of measurable evangelistic goals. In the next year the churches' combined membership went from 2,181 to 3,687, and the churches' growth rate went from 60 percent to over 600 percent. This pilot workshop was repeated fifty-eight times from 1973 to 1978 in forty-three countries. His book, *God's Way to Keep a Church Going and Growing,* was later published in almost sixty languages and became a model for American church growth workshops as well.

Using the basic principles of diagnostic research, each workshop would have the pastor evaluate his church growth patterns and then extend his vision into the future by making "faith projections." According to Gerber, "The most exciting thing about this new type of workshop is its adaptation of the faith promise used so successfully in missionary conferences."[20] Three guidelines were given to workshop participants to help set goals for the growth of their churches.

1. Goals must be set in prayer. God will guide in setting goals.
2. Goals must be set in faith. How many new disciples can you trust God for?
3. Goals must be realistic. They must not be pipe dreams or wishful thinking.

Simply stated, "Every goal is a statement of faith," and as a result of these workshops, God rewarded the faith of these pastors. The church has always prospered and profited with pastors and leaders who had visions and dreams. How institutions develop them is another concern.

INSTITUTIONS AND VISIONS AND DREAMS

It has been observed that successful companies today often have a consensus throughout the organization on a set of overall goals or purpose. It is argued that brilliant strategies will fail without basic organizational support. Leadership requires followership. If a leader needs vision to see where to go and charisma to lead others that way, we are back to a basic unresolved question in management theory: How does a leader build and blend institutional and individual goals together to forge a dynamic organization? Some say the answer is to work from the "top down," while others argue the need to work from the "bottom up." (Interestingly enough, Ted Engstrom has said that current management literature keeps alternating between these two approaches.)

Proponents of a strong participatory process in management and in ministry have ably argued in favor of their view. A survey of statements from this perspective might include the following:

1. Goals must be rooted in the individual for him to be self-motivated.
2. If goals are imposed by an authoritarian leadership, the congregation will be passive.
3. Goal-driven organizations that practice participative management improve productivity.
4. The emerging style of leadership today combines goal-driven management and Theory Z, in which traditional, individual decision making is replaced by consensual decision-making styles.

On the other hand, there are those who argue that strong directive leadership steers the organizational ship straight to the goal. Olan Hendrix says some churches are caught up in the trap of excessive group decision making.

As I observe churches and their organizational structures, I encounter quite regularly two theories—one accurate and one inaccurate—that are held tenaciously by church leadership. One theory is that an important part of church growth is group ownership of the goal to grow. That theory is absolutely true. The second theory says that in order for people to own a goal, they must be allowed to vote on it. This theory, on the other hand, is absolutely false.[21]

How people vote on this controversial issue is the crux of much church organizational conflict and the source of church splits or organizational paralysis. Because this issue is so important, I would like to offer a brief explanation of my perspective on this problem.

Viable Leadership. The answer to this basic organizational question in management theory is dependent on two factors. The first factor is *the minister-manager.* What is his leadership style on the spectrum of director, socializer, relator, or thinker? What is his thinking style on the spectrum of pathfinder to problem-solver, to people-mover? What are his spiritual gifts on the list of pastor, leader, administrator, etc.? How great is his faith, and does he have the "gift of faith"? In today's terms, is he a leader or a manager, or can he be both?

In the book *The Leader-Manager,* a chapter on "Overarching Goals" provides an example of needed insight into this issue. According to the authors, a leader has two tasks. The first is to establish the purpose of an organization, and the second is to enlist the people of the organization. Again, we need vision and charisma. "Each task requires different sets of skills. The first task demands intuitive and analytical ability . . . the second requires inspirational and selling ability."[22] From their point of view, there are not many leaders who are highly proficient in both skill areas, but even though few are "ambidextrous," they believe these skills can be learned. In church terms, the pastor's style, spiritual gifts, and skill-set will greatly influence his philosophy of ministry and approach to decision making in the church.

A second major factor is *the management milieu.* My typology includes major factors that contribute to a viable, as well as variable, leadership role. Review them: Style, Staff, Structure, Size, Situation, Sight. This is how we account for such different approaches, and, in part, this is why different approaches may be acceptable or not acceptable in a given church. A very interesting book for the minister-manager to read would be *The Empowered Manager,* which addresses again the question of who is in charge of the organization. The author says, "People at the top have tremendous impact, yet we are constantly reminded that, in very practical terms, the inmates run the prison!"[23] Even strong pastoral leadership needs to be sensitive leadership, and that is why management is more of an art than a science. Without denying all I have said thus far, a minister-manager may choose a combination of what might be an individual approach to visions and dreams or more of an institutional approach as exemplified in the following three models.

Management by Objectives. In 1965 George S. Odiorne wrote a book by this title and popularized the MBO approach to planning. In this model, the CEO and his staff decide on the corporate purpose and then lower-level managers set, in their own departments, goals and objectives commensurate with the corporate purpose. The key concept of MBO is a participative process at every level of the organization, so that "ownership" can be achieved and people will be motivated and held accountable for results. Although many variations of the model have developed, its sequential steps are simple:

1. Initiate a planning process
2. Analyze the situation
3. Identify opportunities and obstacles
4. Develop purpose, goals, and objectives
5. Formulate strategies
6. Work out action plans
7. Allocate resources
8. Establish control and review procedures.

By 1974, almost half the Fortune 500 companies were using some form of MBO.

The church has given mixed reviews to the use of this management technique. Authoritarian pastors, as well as Roman Catholic clergymen in one study, were more comfortable with a hierarchial mode of management. Some observed that in principle it was simple enough, but in practice it was hard to implement the model in a voluntary organization. One author made the observation that

> the success of goal-setting techniques is probably directly related to the level of consensus already existing within the particular congregation to which they are applied. . . . A unified goal reflects congregational unity, it does not create it.[24]

Pluralistic churches may have a hard time with participatory processes. Still, the model does have some features which are applicable to a church. One example would be CMOR (Church Management by Objectives and Results), described in the book *Managing Church Groups* as "one system that fits into the overall field of organizational development."[25]

Congregational Goals Discovery Plan. In 1971 the office of Worldwide Evangelism in Depth announced a new program for churches, entitled "Goal-oriented Evangelism in Depth," or GED. Unlike Crusade Evangelism in the fifties, and Saturation Evangelism in the sixties, this was to later be called Body Evangelism in the seventies because it focused on the growth of the local church. (The decade of the eighties might well be focused on Life-style Evangelism.) The new element in this evangelistic strategy was an emphasis on goal-setting, based on research and evaluation, and developed by the congregation. By 1975, hundreds of churches had utilized these techniques. It was not intended to be a man-made strategy for a "bigger and better" church per se, but rather a serious attempt for a congregation to discern the will of God in goals.

According to the original manual for GED, "Every goal of the church must be set in a conscious dependence upon the Lord Jesus Christ." In this model the church board was to evaluate priorities suggested by study groups, and then the whole church was to participate in goal-setting. In an article entitled "Goal Setting Gets Your Church Going," various case studies were given, including one small church that

> took a hard look at themselves and bluntly pinpointed their weaknesses, such as lack of vision for outreach and evangelism, wide-spread failure to show hospitality, and infrequent prayer and Bible study both together and in their homes.[26]

As a result, they established some appropriate, specific goals, and the church grew by leaps and bounds.

In the mid-seventies, I studied five churches that utilized GED and compared this model to Vergel Gerber's approach. I found the following distinctions. Compared to GED, Gerber's workshops were (a) more directive than nondirective, (b) more pastor-focused than people-focused, (c) worked more with inner-organizational structures than extra-organizational task forces, and (d) were more specific in terms of church growth numerical goals than other more general goals. In some cases, I felt that weak leadership tended to water down the greatness or strategic development of goals in a congregational consensus decision-making process, but both models had relative merit.

Win Your World for Christ. While at Moody Church I initiated a program to emphasize and encourage Life-style Evangelism. Its stated purpose was to "enable and equip our people to live an effective, evangelistic life-style in their world." It involved a four-point plan beginning with *prayer.* At the beginning of the year, we distributed faith-prayer commitment cards to all of our people with a pulpit challenge to prayerfully make a list of unsaved relatives and friends that they would pray for that year.

The second point was *preparation.* During the year we provided sermons, seminars, and special Sunday school study series to stimulate people to soul-winning and witnessing.

The third point was *programs.* The intention here was to have groups within the church develop their own programs in keeping with our purpose.

The fourth point was *promotion.* All during that year, people were encouraged to return "Evangelistic Prayer Report Cards" so we could publicly praise the Lord for what He had done. Many Sundays we had a "witness stand" in the morning service, where testimonies were shared by people who had witnessed in their world for Christ, and there were even testimonies by some who had been won to the Lord in the process.

Certain principles governed my own thinking about this program. First of all, it was up to leadership, both staff and elders, not only to endorse a "mission statement," but also to be a model of it in their own lives. Second, I wanted the individuals in the church to be involved so the personal prayer commitments of people were turned in as an expression of that "ownership." Third, we as a staff took responsibility to prepare people for the task and promoted it from the pulpit and in special times of prayer. Fourth, I wanted the groups of the church to share ownership through their own plans and programs. I discovered the weakest link in the chain was the need for stronger supervision and suggestions to help group leaders lead. Many lives were touched by our evangelistic efforts, and I learned leadership lessons in the process. Obviously there are many ways to work at helping people in a church "Win Your World for Christ." This is simply a sample of what might be done.

Recently *Fortune* magazine had an article entitled, "Wanted: Leaders Who Can Make a Difference." It said, "The new paragon is an executive who can envision a future for his organization and inspire colleagues to join him in building that future.[27] In the business world, they are still looking for men with vision and charisma. In the believer's world, God is always looking for men with visions and dreams to build His church. I pray we minister-managers will have biblical eyesight to see what God would have us do in our ministries for Him.

NOTES

1. Tom Peters and Nancy Austin, *A Passion for Excellence: The Leadership Difference* (New York: Random House, 1985), 34.
2. Warren Bennis and Burt Nanus, *Leaders: The Strategies for Taking Charge* (New York: Harper & Row, 1985), 89.
3. Craig R. Hickman and Michael L. Silva, *Creating Excellence* (New York: New American Library, 1984), 158-159.
4. Ibid., 51.
5. Mark B. Roman, "The Mission: Setting Your Vision in Words Is the Crucial Executive Act,"*Success,* June 1987, 54-55.

6. Ted W. Engstrom and Edward Dayton, "Having Visions—Dreaming Dreams," *Christian Leadership Letter,* January 1982, 3.
7. Richard R. Broholm, *Strategic Planning for Church Organizations* (Valley Forge, Penn.: Judson, 1969), 18, 29.
8. Jack W. Hayford, "Why I Don't Set Goals," *Leadership,* Winter 1984, 51.
9. Henry Mintzberg, "Planning on the Left Side and Managing on the Right Side," *Harvard Business Review* 54, July-August 1976, 66-67.
10. Daniel J. Isenberg, "How Senior Managers Think," *Harvard Business Review* 52, November-December 1974, 86.
11. Harold J. Leavitt, *Corporate Pathfinders: How Visionary Managers Use Imaginative Strategies to Shape the Future of Their Companies* (New York: Viking Penguin, Penguin Books, 1986), 61.
12. Terrance Hines, "Left Brain, Right Brain: Who's on First?" *Training and Development Journal* 39, November 1985, 32-33.
13. Robert F. Kelley, *The Gold Collar Worker: Harvesting the Brain Power of the New Workforce* (Reading, Mass.: Addison-Wesley, 1985), 59.
14. James G. Bennet and James E. Pravitz, *The Miracle of Sports Psychology* (Englewood Cliffs, N.J.: Prentice-Hall, 1982), 57.
15. Dave Hunt and T. A. McMahon, *The Seduction of Christianity* (Eugene, Ore.: Harvest House, 1986), 143.
16. Harold L. Fickett, *Hope for the Church* (Glendale, Calif.: Regal Books, 1972), 113.
17. C. Peter Wagner, *Your Spiritual Gifts* (Glendale, Calif.: Regal Books, 1979), 158.
18. Jerry Falwell and Elmer Towns, *Stepping Out on Faith* (Wheaton, Ill.: Tyndale House, 1984), 149.
19. Ibid., 11-12.
20. Vergil Gerber, "On Your Mark, Get Set, Grow!" *Moody Monthly,* February 1974, 62.
21. Olan Hendrix, "The Heads and Tails of Decision Making," *Church Growth America,* March-April 1979, 3.
22. David Bradford and Allan Cohen, "Overarching Goals," *The Leader-Manager,* ed. John N. Williamsburg (New York: John Wiley, 1986), 270.
23. Peter Block, *The Empowered Manager: Positive Political Skills at Work* (San Francisco: Jossey-Bass, 1987), xiv.
24. Richard G. Hutchinson, Jr., *Wheel Within the Wheel* (Atlanta: John Knox, 1979), 212.
25. Norman M. Lambert, *Managing Church Groups* (Dayton: Pflaum Publishing, 1975), 3.
26. Paul Heidbrecht and Arnold Swanson, "Goal Setting Gets Your Church Going," *Moody Monthly,* June 1975, 26.
27. Jeremy Main, "Wanted: Leaders Who Can Make a Difference," *Fortune,* 26 September 1987, 92.

CONCLUSION

The supreme task of the church is summed up in the final words of Christ to His apostles in Matthew 28:18-20. It is the Great Commission to make disciples of people in the world. As the early church was faithful to "preach Christ and Him crucified," the Lord made them fruitful in the building of His church (Matt. 16:18) by "adding to their number day by day those who were being saved" (Acts 2:47). The first prerequisite for the minister-manager to serve the Lord in the building of His church is to have had a genuine conversion, a divine calling to the ministry, and a deep commitment to church growth and evangelism. Churches that grow have pastors and leaders who want their church to grow and are also willing to pay the price for it.

Some churches and communities are not conducive to growth, and in many cases the fundamental problem is the minister. Not all men in the ministry are really committed to the Great Commission. A few years ago Larry Richards conducted a nationwide survey of five-thousand pastors from diverse denominational backgrounds. When asked to name the greatest needs their churches had for development, only half of them were giving priority to planning and implementing church growth.[1] While fruitfulness is ultimately dependent upon God, God is also depending upon us to be faithful in seeking to reach people for Christ. I would like to conclude this book with seven steps in a process that can lead from faithfulness to greater fruitfulness in evangelism and church growth.

1. *Purposing.* Show me a church that is growing and I can show you a church that has some sense of where it is going. Lack of clear purpose can impede progress. A recently retired executive secretary of a Baptist denomination told me that many churches were not growing because the pastors and their boards could not agree on what the mission of their churches should be. Howard Hendricks of Dallas Theological Seminary was recently quoted by the Institute of American Church Growth as saying, "More failures in the church come about because of an ambiguity of purpose than for any other reason."[2] The Institute also conducted pastors focus groups and found that a number one need among them was for consultants who could help their churches answer basic questions like: Where are we now? Where do we go? and How do we get there?

Many experts in the field have also commented on the positive possibilities of clearly defined purposes and goals. Donald McGavran and Win Arn say a chief characteristic of growing churches is that they set growth goals "owned by the members." M. Wendell Belew says growing churches have a clear purpose and strategy for growth developed together by their leadership. In his study of five hundred Southern Baptist churches and their stages of growth, Hoyt R. Wilson found the third and final stage of growth usually involved churches in conflict over the nature and goals of the church. Growing churches were able to work out a clearly defined purpose and definite goals. In *Hey, That's Our Church,* Lyle Schaller says fast growing churches tend to have a clear self-image and identity and a set of goals to assimilate new members. And finally, Peter Wagner sums it up when he says, "In all of our research and teaching on what we call the philosophy of ministry, we now see that churches which develop a philosophy of ministry and verbalize it, even putting it in writing, are churches that usually have a more dynamic growth pattern."[3] Once some definite purpose for evangelism and church growth has been settled, there are usually six other steps in the process of producing that growth.

2. *Patterning.* As we have discussed, pastors have different God-given "gift mixes" and styles in their ministries. Not all pastors have "the gift of evangelism (Eph. 4:12), but Paul's counsel to timid Timothy as a pastor to "do the work of an evangelist" (2 Tim. 4:5) and be an example to the church is applicable to *every* minister-manager. It has sometimes been said that the fire of evangelism is more caught than taught, and the pastor should provide a pattern for his people in this regard. In a 1981 study of several hundred Seventh-day Adventist churches, a definite correlation was found between positive growth patterns and five factors. These included higher goals for church growth, an evangelistic purpose in all their activities, a concentrated effort and planning, and a number of members who attended classes on witnessing or leading Bible studies. But first and foremost on the list was "the pastor's personal priority on personal soul-winning."[4]

Elmer Towns, who has written much about America's fastest growing churches, makes the point that in these churches the pastors are personal evangelists as well as pulpit evangelists. An effective pastor never asks his people to make evangelistic calls he is not willing to make himself. I recall one pastor at my church in 1975 when we hosted a local church evangelism conference. He said he loved to be with his people, and he left the conference early to lead them in Saturday afternoon house-to-house calls. Whether or not a pastor has the gift of evangelism—and those who do must be careful not to be competitive or critical of those who don't—his heart concern for people to know Christ needs to be expressed as an example to others.

3. *Praying.* Scripture shows that the early church advanced the gospel through prayer. Although not much evidence is available for any man-made sophisticated strategies, Paul's personal vision to reach Asia was redirected by the Spirit who sent him to Macedonia according to God's plan. Paul's passion (Rom. 9:1-3) for evangelistic preaching (Rom. 10:9-17) was pursued with prayer (Rom. 10:1-2).

Eminent church growth strategist Donald McGavran is very clear on this point, saying, "A church may have all the factors which lead to fruitfulness yet, not seeking the blessing of God, remain barren. Prayer for spiritual infilling has again and again played an important part in the growth of the church. Churches that grow are churches that seek earnestly the gracious power of God."[5] There is no need to develop a dichotomy though between agonizing and organizing, between the Spirit and strategy, or between prayer and planning.

While I was Secretary of Evangelism and Church Growth for the Baptist General Conference in 1979, we placed a major denominational emphasis on evangelistic prayer for growth. People were asked to make a commitment to pray daily for unsaved friends and relatives. Recorded results were rewarding. One church prayed for a woman who had no interest in spiritual things, but the next morning she called a member on the phone to ask questions about the Lord. A pastor's wife made a special plea for a lady in her neighborhood Bible Study, and the next time they met, she led her to Christ. Even young people got involved. One pastor's young daughters included two school friends on their prayer lists, and a few days later they both accepted Christ in the church's girls club program.

I shall never forget one pastor who had people bring copies of their commitments to church at the beginning of that year to lay their lists on the altar for God. During that year, week after week, I would hear stories of people being saved at his church. While I was visiting churches in his area that fall, I said to him, "How many now, John?" He joyfully answered that over two hundred people had come to Christ as God had answered their evangelistic prayers. "We reminded our people in our program that even in church growth and evangelism we may 'have not because we ask not'" (James 4:2).

4. *Preaching.* While preaching by itself may not build great churches, most growing churches have good preachers. Preaching has often been a neglected theme in church growth discussions. In one study of six churches in California's San Gabriel Valley, the leadership interviewed in all of these churches said strong biblical preaching was a chief reason for their growth.

In seminars, I often talk about "The Sales and Service Departments of the Church." As an illustration, I share the results of a study of three large churches in California which had different pastoral styles and views but similarly good growth patterns. The first question in the study was, What caused you to come to this church? (the "Sales Department"). At least 75 percent or more of the people came because a friend or a relative invited them. The second question was, What caused you to *continue* in this church? (the "Service Department"). At least 50 percent of the time it was because of the pastor and his pulpit ministry of God's Word.

Recently I came across an article that raised the question, Is the Pulpit a Factor in Church Growth? The author, Earl Comfort, is pastor of a New Jersey church that grew from three-hundred to twelve-hundred in ten years. In surveys he constructed with similar questions he found the aggregate total of responses for sermons showed that they were the most significant factor for continued church growth. He thereby concluded that "at the heart of growth is an effective pulpit ministry!"[6] The sermons of an effective pulpit ministry were described as being (a) biblical, (b) understandable, (c) warm, (d) positive, (e) practical, (f) exciting, and (g) exemplary.

Preaching the Word of God was very foundational to New Testament church growth. Acts 6:7 says, "The word of God kept on spreading; and the number of the disciples continued to increase greatly." Acts 19:18, 20 says, "Many also of those who had believed kept coming. . . . So the word of the Lord was growing mightily and prevailing."

5. *Preparing.* While the New Testament church had no special training materials (and was still effective!), it did portray a training model expressed by Paul to Timothy when he said, "The things which you have heard from me in the presence of many witnesses, these entrust to faithful men, who will be able to teach others also" (2 Tim. 2:2). Many of the leaders of the New Testament church learned maturity and ministry through "mentorship."

Sometimes people learn to share their faith through a one-on-one personal relationship. I recall one eager church planter in Arizona who would make three hundred calls every Saturday afternoon. His marketing method was simple. First, he called to introduce himself and offered the church brochure to those who would take them. Then he asked if he could put those people on the mailing list. Then he offered a four-week Bible study in the home. New converts were taken out on the Saturday afternoons that followed to learn how to share their faith, particularly with those in their network of unsaved family members and friends.

There are also many other training models today that provide a program with materials and a prepared approach. These programs have been classified "confrontational" evangelism because they usually involve "cold contact" or "initial contact" presentations of the gospel. In 1980 the Evangelical Free Church reported that 25 to 33 percent of their churches had visitation programs for lay evangelism training. Approximately two-thirds of them called on church visitors, while only one-third of them tried "cold contact" calls. Prior to that, in 1978, Warren Bathke studied visitation evangelism in the Free Church and drew some interesting conclusions. First of all, he found a definite correlation between growth patterns and the mobilization of laity for evangelism. While the average size church without a program was about seventy members, churches with programs were about twice the size. (To what extent size influenced the ability to have a program was not discussed.) Second, while only 5 percent of the membership was involved, those churches with the programs had annual growth rates of about 14 percent as compared to other Free Churches without the programs, which had average rates of growth at about 2.6 percent. Bathke's research underscored the value of such programs, although he candidly said that "many pastors are ready to confess that starting and keeping a program going is one of their most difficult tasks."[7]

Some people have criticized these programs because lasting results in the lives of converts seem relatively small. But I have seen many people take these training programs with the results that many contacts for the gospel have been made, and these Christians in the process have gained more confidence, competence, and courage to witness elsewhere. Still, I think pastors today need to emphasize "relational" evangelism training. This is sometimes called Life-style Evangelism and has been popularized by people such as Joe Aldrich, Leighton Ford, Becky Pippert, and the Christian Businessman's Committee, to name a few. They show that in an increasingly secular world more time is needed to cultivate uncompromising relationships with unbelievers before an effective presentation of the gospel may be made. With the general decline of confidence in the church (as seen most recently in the world of tele-evangelism), fewer people come to churches to hear the gospel. More than ever, we need Christians to be witnesses in their world for Christ.

6. *Programming.* Just as there are many different models of training for evangelism, there are many more methods of evangelism that may be more or less effective depending upon the situation. Here again, research shows a positive correlation between programming and positive growth. In a study of some British Baptist churches, those with three or four evangelistic programs had a 9 percent growth pattern per year, while those with five or more had an 11 percent growth pattern. Pastors on Towns's list of fastest growing churches usually had a priority on reaching people for Christ. A church may either develop special programs for their evangelism or infuse their existing program with an evangelistic intent.

Dr. Donald McGavran, church growth strategist, and the late J. Edwin Orr, revival specialist, used to debate in seminary class the relative merits of each approach. Is evangelism the spontaneous result of revival? It can be, but it has not always proved to be. Can evangelism be structured and have the power of the Spirit direct it? Of course, but programs without the Spirit's power and the people's personal commitment may also fail. Like anything else, there must be a biblical balance between what we do for Him and what He does through us.

Some programs try to get people to grow before they go. But discipleship programs don't always lead to spontaneous evangelism. Another approach is to get people to go and, in the process, they will grow. The reflex action of evangelism may lead to revival, or the resulting action of revival may lead to evangelism. So long as our models include going and growing, then programming can make a positive contribution toward people coming to know Christ.

7. *Planning.* Who has not heard the cliché "Plan your work, then work your plan"? And who has not seen the sign with the last letters squeezed at the end, "Plan Ahead!" Research shows that organizations that plan well will usually be more successful than those that do not plan ahead. In addition, those that follow up their plans are more successful than those who do not. James Hayes, president of the American Management Association, said, "Any organization that doesn't plan for its future isn't likely to have one."

Planning can be informal or formal, short-range or long-range, simple or sophisticated, maintenance-oriented or mission-oriented, and, in the process, more or less effective for evangelism. The size, situation, and sophistication of the church will affect the way in which planning is processed. But most churches, when they plan, seem to focus more on efficiency than effectiveness because they have no church growth visions and dreams. They remind me of the story of a young army corporal who came to a canal filled with water and became confused over what command to give. Afraid his squad would march right into the water, he couldn't remember the command "Mark time," so he frantically yelled to his squad, "Quick march—but don't go anywhere!" There is a great deal of difference between marking time and marching forward for Christ in the church.

In conclusion, I would like to share a personal testimony about a special time in my ministry when God granted growth to my church. Some years ago I was the district chairman for a year of denominational emphasis on evangelism and was exercised in heart about the growth of my own church as well. One morning, as I was praying about these matters and reading the Scriptures, I was deeply impressed with the fact that in the early church the Lord added *daily* to the church. The Spirit of God seemed to press the question to my own heart. Would I really like to see that occur in my ministry? My response was affirmative. But then I was also impressed with a more profound question: Could I believe God for one person per day to come to Christ through the combined ministry of my church? I hesitated. I struggled. With a church of two hundred members or so, and not enough evangelistic outreach, I was doubtful. But as I prayerfully considered this challenge from the Lord, I finally made a personal faith commitment to believe God for at least one person per week to come to Christ.

Although I did not announce this to my people, I did make it my aim all year long to pray about, promote, practice, and program evangelism. That year I kept records of all known conversions through home Bible studies, vacation Bible school, Sunday school, personal evangelism, a coffee house ministry, and pulpit invitations. I was so pleased that in my annual report the next year I informed the congregation that God had not given us 52 professions of faith, but exactly 104.

As we are faithful, God will make us fruitful in church growth and in evangelism. As we go, He will cause His church to grow. Jesus said in John 15:16, "I chose you, and appointed you, that you should go and bear fruit, and that your fruit should remain, that whatever you ask of the Father in My name, He may give to you." My prayer is that He will enable you to be a more effective minister-manager in the growth of His church.

NOTES

1. Larry Richards, *Interchange Newsletter,* Vol. 1, No. 5.
2. Win Arn, *The Win Arn Growth Report,* No. 18.
3. C. Peter Wagner, "Taking the Mystery Out of Church Growth," *Commonlife* (Grace Fellowship of Mansfield, Ohio), 1986, 5.
4. Roger L. Dudley, "How Churches Grow," *Ministry,* July 1981, 4-7.
5. Donald McGavran, *How Churches Grow* (New York: Harper & Row, 1954), 57.
6. Earl A. Comfort, "Is the Pulpit a Factor in Church Growth?" *Bibliotheca Sacra* 140, January-March 1983, 64-70.
7. Warren E. Bathke, "Visitation Evangelism: Do We Need It?" *The Evangelical Beacon,* 11 July, 1 August, and 15 August 1978; see article 2, page 11.